My Brother and I

© Joachim Boepple

Andreas Steinhöfel, geboren 1962, arbeitet als Übersetzer, Rezensent und schreibt Drehbücher – vor allem aber ist er Autor zahlreicher, vielfach preisgekrönter Kinder- und Jugendbücher, wie z.B. »Die Mitte der Welt«. Für »Rico, Oscar und die Tieferschatten« erhielt er u.a. den Deutschen Jugendliteraturpreis, den Katholischen Kinder- und Jugendbuchpreis, die Corine und die Auszeichnung »Lesekünstler 2009«. Nach Peter Rühmkorf, Loriot, Robert Gernhardt und Tomi Ungerer hat Andreas Steinhöfel 2009 den Erich Kästner Preis für Literatur verliehen bekommen.

Andreas Steinhöfel

My Brother and I

Ins Englische übersetzt von Chantal Wright

CARLSEN

Außerdem von Andreas Steinhöfel im Carlsen Verlag lieferbar:
Beschützer der Diebe
David Tage Mona Nächte
Defender
Der mechanische Prinz
Die Mitte der Welt
Dirk und ich
Es ist ein Elch entsprungen
Froschmaul – Geschichten
O Patria Mia!
Paul Vier und die Schröders
Rico, Oskar und die Tieferschatten
Rico, Oskar und das Herzgebreche
Trügerische Stille

Für Christian und Steffen

Veröffentlicht im Carlsen Verlag
Juli 2011

Lektorat: Georgia Murray
Vokabelteil: Laura Hoppe
Umschlagbild: Regina Kehn
Umschlaggestaltung: formlabor
Corporate Design Taschenbuch: Dörte Dosse
Gesetzt aus der Bembo von Dörlemann Satz, Lemförde
Druck und Bindung: GGP Media GmbH, Pößneck
ISBN 978-3-551-31062-0
Printed in Germany

Alle Bücher im Internet: www.carlsen.de

Contents

Let It Snow

The first snowfall of the year came at the beginning of December, on a Saturday.

That morning, Dirk and I went into the kitchen where Mum and Dad were already sitting at the breakfast table. Dad didn't have to work on Saturdays because the bank where he was **in charge of** a department was closed. Mum worked as a secretary in Braun's large factory, but only part-time. She was always telling people that she needed the rest of the time **to clean up the mess** we and Dad made in the flat.

So Mum was sitting with Dad at the breakfast table with both her hands placed comfortably on her **sticky-out belly** where the baby was. Look out of the window, she said, the outdoors has put on its white coat.

Dirk and I went over to the window and looked out. Dirk said he couldn't see a coat, but there was snow everywhere and wasn't that fantastic because now we could go sledging and build snowmen.

---

to be in charge of something – für etwas verantwortlich sein

to clean up the mess – die Unordnung beseitigen, den Dreck aufräumen

sticky-out belly – *Kindersprache*: hervorstehender Bauch

Tons of snowflakes were falling from the sky, millions and millions of them. I picked out one that was still a long way up and watched it until it lay on the ground with the others.

We were still living in the house on the edge of town then. Dad's aunt, the one we **inherited** the house *in* town from, hadn't died yet. Björn wasn't born either, he didn't arrive until the next April. I didn't have my **guinea pig** Fran yet either, and I only met Behruz, the fat Persian who would become my friend, much later.

But Richard was already my best friend. We were true blood brothers.

I was seven years old and Dirk was six.

Anyway, because of all the fresh snow that day, Dirk and I wanted to go sledging after breakfast.

Dad brought our sledge down from the attic. He told us **not to go mad** and break the thing, the way we did last year when Dirk had crashed into a tree and broken his arm.

Dirk was always much **braver** than I was, but then again I'd never broken anything. Apart from one summer when I had sort of ridden into a street lamp on my bike. I'd knocked out two teeth and swallowed them. But it wasn't all that bad **cos** they were only milk teeth.

---

to inherit – erben
guinea pig – Meerschweinchen
not to go mad – *hier*: es nicht übertreiben
brave – mutig
cos – *umgangssprachlich für*: because – weil

While Dad was fetching the sledge, Mum wrapped us up in warm clothes. We had to wear gloves and our bobble hats. Finally, Mum wrapped the big thick scarves that Granny had knitted for us around our necks.

Granny was Mum's mum. There was usually trouble when she came to visit because Dad **couldn't stand her**. Granny always told us that Dad had been a real **yob** in his youth. He used to drive around on his motorbike scaring all the old people and she would never understand why Mum had married such an idiotic show-off.

Granny liked to tell stories of the old days. Her favourite stories were all about how she had run through the bombed-out ruins of the town after the war carrying Aunt Gertrud on her back. I always felt sorry for her when she told us that, cos Aunt Gertrud was really really fat.

Dad's mum had died before Dirk and I were born and we didn't have any grandads either.

So Mum wrapped the scarves around our necks and told us to be very careful and not to go breaking any bones or teeth again. And then we were finally allowed to go.

Only fifteen minutes away from our house there was a big field with a really long **slope** that led all the way down to the stream. That's where Dirk and I were going.

The snow was piled up quite high and when we got to

---

couldn't stand her – konnte sie nicht ausstehen
yob – Halbstarker, Flegel
slope – *hier*: Schlittenbahn

the field it was still snowing. It was very cold and quiet everywhere. The only sound came from the snowflakes falling quietly on to the ground and from our boots stomping through the snow. We climbed up the slope and I pulled the sledge after me.

When we reached the top, Dirk wanted to slide down the steepest bit of course, the bit that led to the stream. Right away I thought that things were bound to go wrong, but I didn't say anything so that Dirk wouldn't think I was a **wimp**.

We sat down on the sledge. Dirk at the front and me at the back.

Hold tight, cried Dirk, here we go!

It was fantastic, and above all fantastically fast. The wind whooshed around my ears, snowflakes smacked into my face and I could **hardly** see anything because I had screwed my eyes up tight. We went faster and faster and Dirk shouted out that he was the best sledger in the world and I shouted out, when were we finally going to get there because I couldn't see a thing.

Then there was a bang.

I sailed briefly through the air, there was a crash and I landed with my face down in the snow. It **hurt** a lot and I felt hot, but at least I didn't have any broken bones.

---

wimp – Feigling
hardly – kaum
to hurt – schmerzen

Dirk wasn't there. Neither was the sledge.

I looked around and then I heard Dirk shouting up from the stream.

He was sitting right in the middle of it, with the sledge next to him, **soaked** to the skin. Thank God the stream wasn't particularly deep there. But the bank was quite high, at least a metre tall.

I had to laugh, because Dirk looked so funny with his wet bobble hat on his head. But he was really mad and yelled at me that he didn't see what was so funny, I hadn't steered properly, I was an idiot and in future I should stay at home and build snowmen.

I yelled back, idiot yourself, you're too stupid to go sledging, and I said that if he didn't **keep his trap shut**, then he could find his own way out of the stream.

Dirk called back that I could go ahead and leave him all alone, then he'd freeze and there'd be no Christmas and probably no New Year either because everybody would be in **mourning**.

I pretended to think about it, and then I said, all right, I'll get you out – but only because of Christmas!

I held on to the branch of a small tree that was hanging over the stream with one hand. I stretched the other hand down to Dirk. I couldn't quite reach and it was slippy be-

---

soaked – klatschnass
to keep one's trap shut – die Klappe halten
mourning – Trauer

cause of the snow but the branch didn't break. Dirk grabbed my hand and everything would have been fine if he hadn't leaned over towards the sledge without letting go of me, the **meanie**.

The branch made a cracking noise and snapped, and I fell down the bank into the stream. I would have screamed but my mouth was already full of water. It was icy cold. I was so shocked I could hardly breathe.

When I had picked myself up, Dirk was standing next to me laughing himself to bits. I was so **cross** that I slapped him with my wet glove. Dirk stopped laughing, slapped me back and before we knew it we were both in the water fighting. If it hadn't been so freezing cold, we would probably have fought a lot longer, but we just couldn't.

We had to run downstream for quite a long time until we found a spot where we could climb out. By then it had stopped snowing, but it was windy and we were shivering with cold.

I was afraid that the two of us would freeze to death and stand there like **icicles**. Nobody would **recognise** us in our frozen state and Mum and Dad would have to call the police and ask them to search for us. It would take months until they found us and by then it would be spring, and in the meantime every single passing dog would have

---

meanie – Fiesling
to be cross – sauer sein, böse sein
icicle – Eiszapfen
to recognise – wiedererkennen

weed on us because they thought we were bushes covered in snow.

I really wanted to cry, but if I did my eyes might freeze shut. It was terrible and then on top of everything Dirk **wet his pants**.

When we got home, Mum was really mad. She took off our wet things and put us into a really hot bath. Mum said, because you're so stupid and can't take care of yourselves, I am **banning** sledging for the whole of the next week.

Dirk started to cry but I thought, well, the stupid sledge is stuck in the stream anyway. And that's what I told Dad when he asked about the sledge and then he was cross too. He said we only had ourselves to blame if we were only allowed to build snowmen for the whole of the following week.

But he went to fetch the sledge while Mum put Dirk and I in our pyjamas and made us a bed on the couch in the living room. She even gave us a hot water bottle for our feet. She grinned and said that we were stupid but that she loved us nonetheless and that was why she was going to make us hot chocolate.

When Dad had returned with the sledge, Dirk and I had to tell Mum and Dad exactly how we had landed in the stream and how we had got into a fight and everything.

Well, said Dad, something similar had happened to him

---

to wet one's pants – sich in die Hose machen
to ban something – etwas verbieten

when he was young. And he told us how, when he was a kid, he had landed in the village pond while sledging with his brother, Uncle Alfred. They had run over a duck on the frozen pond before crashing into the ice and the duck had fallen into the hole and **drowned** and never come back up again.

Mum said, Peter! Don't tell the children such horrible things!

Dad said, *that* wasn't horrible. The horrible thing was that the duck's mate, the **drake**, was so **distraught** at the loss of his beloved that he had thrown himself into the hole after her. And the year after that, a bush had grown out of the pond in the shape of two ducks kissing, and ducks from all over the country had come to the pond and swum around in a circle quacking.

That's what happened, said Dad and drank some of his hot chocolate.

Quack, quack, said Dirk. And he flapped his eyes as though he wanted to fly. He knocked over his cup and the chocolate spilled all over our **blanket**.

Men! said Mum. She rolled her eyes, put one hand on her sticky-out tummy and laughed.

Two days later Dirk and I were allowed to go sledging again.

---

to drown – ertrinken
drake – Erpel
to be distraught – verzweifelt sein, außer sich sein
blanket – Decke

It's the Most Wonderful Time of the Year

It was the week before Christmas. Dirk and I had a great idea.

There was an old people's home really close to our house. We walked past it every day on our way home from school. It was **on the edge of town** and really big, with lots of windows and tall trees in front of it. And next to the old people's home there was a tall building. That's where the penguins lived.

Really they're called **nuns**, but we called them penguins because they wore black clothes and white bonnets on their heads. When it rained they put see-through plastic bags over their bonnets and then they really did look funny.

The penguins made sure that none of the old people ran away from the home. I couldn't stand them. Whenever we met them on our way home, they told us about the Baby Jesus and they looked all holy.

I thought the Baby Jesus was OK, but the penguins wanted us to be just like him, really nice and everything.

---

on the edge of town – am Stadtrand
nun – Nonne

That's why they gave us little **leaflets** with stupid pictures inside and sayings like »love your enemy« and »it's really great to give things to people who don't have anything«. Why should I give my electric train set to some idiot who might be about to hit me, just because he doesn't have one of his own? What a stupid idea!

Anyway, back to the old people's home. That's where all the grannies and grandads lived. And Dirk and I thought that because it was nearly Christmas, we could visit them and make little presents for them and sing them songs. We wanted to spend an afternoon making things and go to the old people's home the next afternoon with our presents.

Mum thought it was a great idea and promised to bake special Christmas biscuits for us to eat while we were making things.

It would have been fantastic if my blood brother Richard could have **joined in**, but he had gone skiing with his parents. So I asked Susanne, who was my best friend, if she wanted to join in.

Susanne had said, all right, but only if her friend Christiane could join in too.

Christiane was in our class as well.

And I said, OK then, if she really had to. But I was actually very excited, because I was in love with Christiane

---

leaflet – Heftchen, Faltblatt
to join in – mitmachen

and wanted to marry her. But Dirk was the only one who knew about it and he had sworn not to tell anybody.

Susanne and Christiane came on the agreed afternoon at three o'clock.

Christiane looked great. She had long black hair that was always in a plait or a pony tail. Today it was in a pony tail.

Susanne had short brown hair and **braces** on her teeth and thick glasses.

We started work right away because we didn't know exactly how many people lived in the old people's home and so we wanted to make quite a lot of presents.

Mum filled a giant tray with biscuits. She put it down on the table. She lit the candles on the advent wreath and it was really cosy.

We made lots of stars from coloured paper, and gold and silver ones from foil. We made small **necklaces** too, using string and shiny **beads**, and then some more stars out of straws.

Mum said we could practise our **Christmas carols** while we were working.

Dirk wanted to show off and started singing *'Tis the season to be jolly*, but because he had a big piece of biscuit in his mouth, he choked. His head went really red and he

---

braces – Zahnspange
necklace – Halskette
bead – Perle
Christmas carols – Weihnachtslieder

made strange noises. Mum didn't look all that jolly any more. She clapped Dirk hard on the back and stuck her fingers down his throat. Maybe Dirk thought she had stuck another biscuit in there. In any case he **chomped down** on her fingers.

Mum screamed, but she didn't let go and suddenly the piece of biscuit was back out again, covered in a lot of spit.

At first we were all frightened. But then we laughed and Dirk laughed too. He rolled his eyes and made a gurgling noise as though he still had biscuit stuck in his throat.

Then we sang some more Christmas carols and Susanne sounded funny because of her braces. In between singing we **scoffed** the biscuits. We worked until it had gone dark outside and in the end we had a whole box full of presents.

I said I would dress up as Saint Nick and that way we could put all the presents into a proper sack.

Susanne said that was a good idea, and that she would be the Christ Child.

And that's when we started to **argue**.

Dirk wanted to be the Christ Child too, but Susanne said, you're crazy, the Christ Child is a girl with long blonde curls.

Dirk said, first of all Susanne didn't have blonde curls, and secondly the Christ Child had a willy, so he was a boy.

---

to chomp down – zubeißen
to scoff – sich vollstopfen mit
to argue – streiten

But Christiane said the Christ Child *was* a girl, but she had long black hair and no braces and she didn't wear silly cow glasses and that's why Christiane had to be it.

Dirk said, rubbish, the Christ Child doesn't have blonde hair or black hair, he's **bald**, and he **definitely** has a willy. But by then Susanne had already hit Christiane because she had said silly cow glasses.

Christiane picked up one of the biscuits and threw it at Susanne's head and Susanne smacked her with one of the pearl necklaces. If Mum hadn't stepped in, the two of them would probably have broken all the presents.

Mum said none of this was a problem, there would just have to be two Christ Childs and two Saint Nicks and the second Saint Nick would be Dirk.

Dirk said, all right then, but the Christ Child did have a willy and he would only dress up as Saint Nick because he didn't want to shave his hair off.

Susanne and Christiane **grumbled** for a bit longer, but by the time Mum took them home later, they were friends again.

The next day Dirk and I were really excited.

We looked fantastic dressed up as Saint Nicks. Mum had given us her and Dad's red dressing gowns. We put them on over our proper clothes. They were a bit too long and

---

bald – kahlköpfig
definitely – eindeutig, bestimmt
to grumble – meckern, grummeln

dragged along the floor. They didn't have any **hoods** either, so we put our bobble hats on. Our hats weren't red, unfortunately, they were blue with green in them, but they were better than nothing. We had stuck on beards made of cotton wool and Mum had painted our cheeks red with lipstick, which looked great. The presents were packed very carefully in a proper potato sack so that they didn't **get squashed**.

Then Christiane and Susanne arrived.

Christiane's mum had sewn her a proper white dress out of an old bed sheet and she had curls in her black hair and a golden crown on top of her head. It was a brilliant costume and I was even more in love with her than I had been before.

Susanne didn't look quite right dressed as the Christ Child. She was wearing a blonde wig with long curls that hung over her glasses. Her dress was also made out of a bed sheet but it wasn't sewn properly, it was just **draped around** her. But even worse than that were the two cardboard wings she had fastened to the sheet on her back. Plus she was wearing red **wellies** and I felt really sorry for her because she looked so silly.

But Susanne loved her costume and Mum said we were the best Saint Nicks and Christ Childs she had ever seen.

Then, finally, we set off.

---

hood – Kapuze
to get squashed – zerquetscht werden
draped around – *hier*: umgehängt
wellies – Gummistiefel

Instead of going down the street, we took **a short cut** through the woods. It only took ten minutes but we had to stomp our way through all the snow. I carried the sack with the presents on my back.

The woods looked beautiful. All of the trees were white. Now and then small clumps of snow fell off branches. We had almost reached the old people's home when Dirk said that Saint Nick needed a staff.

Susanne said we could take some twigs off a tree. She stood under a big fir tree and said, this one will do.

Dirk and I stood next to Susanne and Dirk pulled at a small branch. Snowflakes whirled down but the branch didn't break off. Dirk pulled at a bigger branch. More snowflakes fell and then the branch cracked and a **giant pile** of snow shot off the fir tree.

Most of it landed on Susanne. She had a proper pile of snow on her wig, her sheet had slipped and one wing was dangling down. We tried to **fasten** it back on but it wouldn't stick.

Susanne wasn't too upset and laughed, but Christiane said she looked like a one-legged duck. I thought that was stupid of Christiane, especially because the snow hadn't touched her at all but it had completely covered Susanne and she didn't have to go and make a stupid joke about it.

---

short cut – Abkürzung
a giant pile – ein riesiger Haufen
to fasten – befestigen

Dirk and I had only got a little bit on us. We were able to shake the snow off quite easily.

And now we had a big branch. We broke off two twigs. Those were our Saint Nick staffs and they were fantastic.

And then we went to the old people's home.

At first they didn't want to let us in!

We rang the bell and the penguins didn't open up, even though we sang *Good King Wenceslas* for five minutes, *Sire, the night is darker now and the wind blows stronger.* Nothing happened.

I was just thinking, that's typical, they give out stupid leaflets and talk about Baby Jesus but they let little children freeze at the front door, when there was a **crackling** on the **intercom** and a voice asked us what we wanted.

I said, good afternoon, this is Saint Nick and two Christ Childs and another Saint Nick and we've got some presents for the old people.

For a while nothing happened. Then, finally, the door opened.

One of the penguins looked out and said, well, will you look at that? Come in, children.

By then I didn't want to any more, but it was too late. We went inside, into a large room where lots of penguins were standing around a large Christmas tree.

Everybody grinned at us and said, well, children, will

---

a crackling – ein Knacken, Knistern
intercom – Sprechanlage

you look at that, what are you doing here? Then they all looked at Christiane and cried, well, will you look at that? How sweet, a proper little angel, and Christiane **curtsied** and smiled and shook her black curls.

The penguins thought that was great. But then they asked us once again what we wanted and Dirk got quite cross. He **snapped at** them, couldn't they see who was standing right in front of them and they should take us to the grannies and grandads right away or they'd **get a whack** from the staff.

I thought, oh dear, now they'll throw us out. But the penguins cried out again, oh how sweet! That was irritating and I really would like to have hit them with the staff because they were behaving as though we were tiny babies and **not quite all there**.

But one of them was really nice. She said, well, I'm Sister Erika and I'll show you our old people. I'm sure they'll be very pleased to see you.

We marched up one set of stairs and thank God the other penguins stayed standing in the hallway. One of them came around the corner with a cleaning cloth because the floor was covered in water from where Dirk and I had dragged our dressing gowns behind us.

---

to curtsy – einen Knicks machen
to snap at somebody – jemanden anschnauzen
to get a whack – Prügel bekommen
to be not quite all there – nicht ganz richtig im Kopf sein

Upstairs we went along a long corridor that smelled like a **chemist's** or the dentist's.

Sister Erika gave a quick knock on a door, opened it and said, well, Mrs Sommer, look who's come to visit, isn't this nice?

We followed her into the room and there was Mrs Sommer lying in bed. She was really old and had **barely** any hair and she shook a little and looked at us. The room was small and dark. There was only a cupboard in there and a chair and a table. There was a plate on the table with a few branches of fir and a candle on it which wasn't lit, and an old photo of a young woman and a young man smiling at each other hung on the wall above.

I felt all **strange**. But Susanne went up to Mrs Sommer and said we had something for her. Then she began to sing, *O Christmas Tree, O Christmas Tree.*

Her braces made it sound like *O Kwissmas Twee, O Kwissmas Twee*, and water ran out of her wig on to the floor and the right half of her cardboard wings dangled down. But Mrs Sommer thought it was great and we sang along.

I unpacked one of the golden stars, a straw star and a pearl necklace and put everything on the blanket. Then Mrs Sommer took my hand in hers and cried a little and I felt really sorry for her.

---

chemist's – Apotheke
barely – kaum
strange – merkwürdig

Sister Erika stood next to her and looked sad too.

When we had finished with the song, she said, right, Mrs Sommer, that was nice, wasn't it, and then we had to leave.

We went into the next room and into the next, along the whole corridor and up to the second floor as well and it looked like Mrs Sommer's everywhere.

Except, some of the old people weren't sick in bed but were wide awake. They talked to us and said the singing and the presents were a great idea. Everyone was **pleased** and some of them sang along. A few of them cried, too.

Christiane shook her curls each time and did curtsies. After a few rooms she didn't sing along any more, which I thought was stupid.

The last room belonged to a married couple.

They used to be teachers, said Sister Erika. The man had a stern expression on his face and stood perfectly straight while we sang a song. His wife stood next to him, but she was a bit more **crooked**.

When we had finished singing, the man said, **jolly good show**, jolly good show! He clapped Dirk and I on the back and smiled.

Christiane curtsied again, and he clapped her and Susanne on the back. Susanne's right wing fell off. His wife

---

to be pleased – sich freuen
they used to be – sie waren mal
crooked – bucklig, gekrümmt
jolly good show – *hier*: gut gemacht

wanted to put it back on again, but it wouldn't stick. So Susanne said the woman could keep it as a souvenir.

She grinned at the woman through her thick glasses and her braces gleamed. The woman leaned over and stroked Susanne's wig and gave her a kiss on the cheek. Christiane looked really **jealous**.

Sister Erika took us back into the corridor. It was already dark outside and my throat was hurting from all the singing. We had a few presents left over. We gave those to the penguins who were standing around in the hallway again staring at us.

Sister Erika said she had something for us because we were such nice children. Then she opened a cupboard that was full of chocolate from top to bottom and gave some to each of us. I thought that was very nice. I really like chocolate and after that I thought Sister Erika really wasn't all that bad at all.

Christiane curtsied again, smiled sweetly and shook her curls with the golden crown on top. And then she said to Susanne that Susanne should hand over her bar of chocolate because Christiane was the prettier Christ Child of the two. She was probably still cross because Susanne had got a kiss and she hadn't, even though she had curtsied non-stop.

But Susanne didn't hand over the chocolate and Christiane suddenly got very angry and pulled off Susanne's bed

---

jealous – eifersüchtig

sheet. Susanne tried to **hang on to it** but she only managed to catch the left cardboard wing and it tore off.

Christiane called out, there, you silly cow, take that! She threw the sheet on to the ground and trampled all over it.

Susanne screamed through her braces, shilly cow yourshelf, and whacked Christiane over the head with her bar of chocolate, **squishing** her golden crown. Then the two of them started to fight and wrestled with each other in front of the chocolate cupboard.

The penguins were completely **horrified** and cried out, but children, it's not nice to fight, the Christ Child wouldn't do such a thing!

Christiane shouted that the Christ Child *would* do such a thing and hit Susanne on the nose.

Susanne began to cry.

Dirk said, are you crazy, and gave Christiane a big push. And then Christiane started to cry that she was the most beautiful Christ Child in the world, not Susanne.

That's not true, Dirk called out, because she wasn't bald and she didn't have a willy, and the penguins **screamed**, good God in heaven!

Whack, Christiane thumped Dirk. She launched herself at him and pulled his bobble hat down over his eyes and then she hit him on the nose, just like Susanne.

---

to hang on to something – etwas festhalten
to squish – *hier*: kaputtschlagen
to be horrified – entsetzt sein
to scream – schreien

The penguins screamed and **huddled together** in a group instead of sorting out the fight.

Dirk shouted from under his bobble hat that I was supposed to help him but obviously I would rather let my brother get hit by a stupid girl just because I was in love with her!

That was **embarrassing**!

But by then Sister Erika had got hold of Christiane and said in a loud voice, that's enough, young lady!

Christiane yelled that she should take her penguin fingers off her and gave her a push. Sister Erika crashed into the Christmas tree.

The tree wobbled, but it didn't fall over. Sister Erika gasped for air. And then she went over to Christiane and **slapped** her.

Everything went suddenly quiet. Nobody made a sound.

Sister Erika asked Christiane for her name, went to the telephone and called her mother to come and **collect** her.

Later Mum spent a long time on the phone with Christiane's mum.

Dirk and Susanne and I sat in the kitchen while she was talking and tried to listen in, but we couldn't.

I thought about Christiane and that now I wasn't in love with her any more. I thought about all the grannies and

---

to huddle together – sich zusammendrängen
embarrassing – peinlich
to slap – schlagen
to collect someone – jemanden abholen

grandads in the old people's home too and how things in the world are sometimes really stupid.

Cos there they were, living in that ugly old people's home, surrounded by penguins who all behaved as though old people were babies. But lots of the old people had children who didn't take care of them, that's what they'd told us. I thought, when Mum and Dad are that old, I won't let them move into an old people's home. They can live with me or with Dirk instead.

Shortly afterwards Mum came into the kitchen. She said Christiane had **behaved so strangely** because she had problems at home. Her parents were **getting divorced**.

Dirk said that made no difference, you still couldn't just **lose your temper** and hit your friends. Mum said perhaps Christiane only did it because she would have liked to hit her parents instead, but she couldn't.

I could understand that. I had once picked a fight with Dirk when Dad had yelled at me for not doing my homework, and it wasn't Dirk's fault.

In any case we all felt sorry for Christiane now. Susanne said, well, maybe they could still be friends.

And I thought Susanne was brilliant with her thick glasses and her braces and we put a candle in the window

---

to behave strangely – sich merkwürdig benehmen
to get divorced – sich scheiden lassen
to lose one's temper – die Beherrschung verlieren

and looked out at the snow falling, hundreds and hundreds of flakes. Then we ate the chocolate and the rest of the biscuits and we sang Christmas carols, *O Kwissmas Twee, O Kwissmas Twee.*

The Spaghetti Monster

When it's your birthday, it feels like Christmas, only better. Christmas is for everyone, but your birthday is just for you and you don't have to sing advent hymns every Sunday for weeks beforehand. My birthday is on the fourteenth of January and it's great getting two presents in a row.

The night before my eighth birthday I was so excited I couldn't sleep properly. That's why I'd been lying awake in bed for a long time before Mum and Dad crept into our room in the morning. Something that rattled and rustled was put down next to my bed but I **pretended** I was still sleeping, even though I was almost bursting with excitement. Mum woke up Dirk. He grumbled that he wanted to sleep a bit longer. I thought, come on, get up, you **lazy bones**! I wanted to shout at him to hurry up and move.

When everybody was finally standing around my bed, I had already planned out how I would pretend that I was only just waking up. I had seen how you do it in a TV advert for coffee: first you toss and turn a little bit and then

---

to pretend – so tun als ob
lazy bones – Faulpelz

you smile and sniff the coffee. Then you throw both your arms in the air and stretch like a cat and keep on smiling. You open your eyes and there's a person standing next to the bed with coffee and a vase full of flowers saying: Good morning, darling. And you answer: What a great morning this is, especially with this wonderful, aromatic, strong coffee. I'm so happy it's **on special offer**. Then the two people give each other a kiss and go swimming or jogging and the coffee sits on the breakfast table at home giving off steam while they're gone.

Simple.

When Mum leaned over me with her sticky-out baby belly and said very quietly, Andy, love, wake up, I started to smile, but only a little bit, and I tossed and turned. Then I sniffed but it didn't smell of coffee, more like a **chicken coop**, which I thought was a bit strange, but I kept on smiling and threw up my arms.

Almost half of my bed lay under the window sill, and my right arm crashed into the flower pot with the ivy that was on top of it. The flower pot fell off the window sill, landed on something metallic and crashed on to the floor. It was very difficult to keep on smiling as though I hadn't noticed anything.

I slowly opened my eyes and saw Mum standing right over me, but she didn't look anything like the person from

---

on special offer – im Sonderangebot
chicken coop – Hühnerstall

the coffee advert and she didn't look as though she wanted to go swimming or jogging with me either. She looked at me and said, congratulations, I had just demolished her **prizewinning super-ivy**, and Dirk trumpeted behind her, yes, and the flower pot had almost squashed my birthday present.

But then everybody shouted, happy birthday, and Mum and Dad gave me a kiss and **hugged** me and Dirk jumped around the room and shouted, look at your present!

Next to the bed, on the floor, was a giant cage. A couple of branches of Mum's super-ivy were hanging over it and a little bit of soil from the flower pot had fallen inside. The cage was full of straw and in between the straw a guinea pig was running up and down excitedly.

Dad laughed and said, poor creature, the flower pot has given it a shock. It'll have a heart attack if it carries on like that.

Mum asked if I'd already thought of a name for it. I thought for a moment and then I said, I'll call him Fran because he's **frantic**.

I opened the cage and lifted Fran up on to the bed. He was pretty small. His fur was brown with white bits and it was really bobbly and he had brown eyes.

---

prizewinning super-ivy – preisgekrönter Super-Efeu
to hug someone – jemanden umarmen
frantic – hektisch, wahnsinnig aufgeregt

Fran sniffed at me and made funny noises. I held him tight between my hands and I could feel his little heart beating really, really fast because he was so excited. His moustache hairs tickled my skin. I thought Fran was great and I said he was the best birthday present I'd ever had.

That afternoon Dirk and I set the table in the kitchen for the children I'd invited to my party, and Mum set the table in the living room for our uncles and aunts, who I *hadn't* invited, but who turned up at every birthday party anyway. Relatives only ever give you silly underpants that are too big for your birthday and they eat all the cake that's meant for the children. At least all my cousins were already grown up and stayed at home. Granny would normally have come, but she'd gone on holiday to a spa because she needed to lose weight again. She had sent me a birthday card with a pink hippo holding a bunch of flowers in one hand, grinning.

In any case, at half past three the party finally started.

I had invited Susanne and Christiane, who were best friends again now. Stefan and Bernd came too. They were twins and like **two peas in a pod** or something. They brought **Chubby** Uli with them, who sat next to me at school.

I was also expecting Richard, but he hadn't come yet and I was really cross.

---

to be like two peas in a pod – sich gleichen wie ein Ei dem anderen
chubby – dick

I got fantastic presents, books and a big **jigsaw** and a giant model ship to make. Susanne had drawn me a picture of us standing in front of the Christmas tree at the old people's home with the penguins, and that was fantastic too.

I got Fran out of his cage and everybody was allowed to take turns holding and stroking him.

Stefan said that guinea pigs must be from Papua New Guinea, and that was an island so they must be able to swim or else how would they have got here and Bernd said, that's right, we could fill the bath up with water and let Fran swim around in a salad bowl like Robinson Crusoe.

I didn't think that was such a great idea because the twins' ideas usually went wrong. Their hamster had once broken a leg because his parachute hadn't opened when they'd thrown him off the balcony.

Uli said **he couldn't care less** whether Fran could swim or not. He'd much rather know if guinea pigs were **edible** and when he was finally going to get a piece of cake.

I didn't really want to cut the cake before Richard arrived, but I was afraid that Uli would actually take a bite out of Fran because he was so hungry. Once, he had drunk a glass full of **frog spawn** and I thought, if he can drink frog spawn, he might eat a small guinea pig too. So we started without Richard.

---

jigsaw – Puzzle
he couldn't care less – es wäre ihm völlig egal
edible – essbar
frog spawn – Froschlaich

We were just playing Simon Says when my relatives arrived with the underpants. The uncles rushed into the living room and up to the drinks cabinet with Dad and the aunts all went into the kitchen. Aunt Marianne, who was one of Mum's sisters and didn't have any children of her own, pulled me down from my chair and squashed me against her big **bosom**, even though my mouth was full of buttercream cake.

She screeched, my, look at how he's grown, our little Andy Pandy, and she held me so tight I almost **puked**.

Uli laughed so hard he spat his piece of marble cake across the table. He shouted, my, look what a cutie he is, our little Andy Pandy, and everybody laughed themselves silly, apart from Christiane, whose left cheek had been hit by the flying piece of half-chewed marble cake.

In revenge she shot a piece of Swiss roll at Uli with her fork, but it flew past him and landed on Aunt Gertrud, Mum's other sister.

Aunt Gertrud was unbelievably small and fat, like a blow-up ball. She was covered with jewellery from head to toe as always and she looked like our Christmas tree which was still standing in the living room, the only difference being that she wasn't wearing little candles. She had a dress on that was pink everywhere, apart from where the Swiss

---

bosom – Busen
to puke – sich übergeben
in revenge – aus Rache

roll had landed. She was cross and was about to start complaining.

Mum said, Gertrud, don't **get wound up**, think about your gall bladder.

Aunt Gertrud forgot about the Swiss roll and started telling everybody about her stupid gall bladder. A gall bladder is some sort of organ that does something with the fat in your body, but not in Aunt Gertrud's case. She went into the living room with Mum, followed by Aunt Marianne and Aunt Erika, Uncle Alfred's wife. Aunt Erika was great. She was the only one who hadn't given me any underpants and had given me a book instead. The book was all about guinea pigs.

After we had eaten our cake we played Blind Man's Buff and Pin the Tail on the Donkey.

It was already dark outside and Richard still hadn't come. I was **getting annoyed** because I thought he had forgotten about my birthday. When we had finished playing Pin the Tail on the Donkey, Uli had a really sore arm where Susanne had tried to pin the tail on him instead of on the donkey. I thought she had done it on purpose because while we were playing Blind Man's Buff, Uli had said that Susanne must be the blindest man of all with her thick glasses and so there was no need to put a **blindfold** on her.

---

to get wound up – sich aufregen
to get annoyed – sich ärgern, sich aufregen
blindfold – Augenbinde

In any case, Uli was clutching his sore arm and crying, and Susanne was saying, not bad for a blind man, when Dad came into the playroom and cried, all right you little monkeys, get dressed, we're going sledging.

Everybody had brought their sledge with them, but we had forgotten all about it and now it was dark outside. I thought, Dad must be crazy if he's going to let us all slide into the stream in the dark so that we drown and he can finally have peace and quiet at home and get drunk with all our relatives.

But Dad was perfectly **serious**. So we put our warm things on, went outside in the dark and pulled our sledges behind us through the snow.

And then came the best surprise of all!

Richard was standing on the sledging field. He had put over forty **torches** into the snow in two lines running down the hill, and the snow was glowing as though a volcano had erupted.

Richard shouted, happy birthday, blood brother! And then he lit a New Year's firework that he had saved especially for my birthday. The firework shot up into the sky and exploded. It looked as though hundreds of thousands of stars were falling to earth from the darkness, and it was so beautiful I almost cried.

I had the best sledge rides of my life. Whenever I shot

---

to be serious – *hier*: es Ernst meinen
torch – Fackel

past one of the torches, the snow shone as though it was covered in red jewels and in the light from the flickering flames it **looked as though** the hill was moving like waves in the sea.

After an hour Dad said we had to go home for dinner. The torches would have burned down soon anyway.

But everybody was allowed to pull one out of the snow and take it with them and on the way home we all sang This Little Light of Mine and I thought, Richard is my best friend in all the world.

Mum had made us spaghetti with sauce for dinner and we were allowed to eat it without forks, just with our hands from the big pot which Mum normally used for making jam. The table, the chairs and the bench in the corner were covered in plastic sheeting and it was an absolute **pigsty** and lots of fun because the sauce splashed everywhere and the spaghetti slapped against your ears if you sucked it up and shook your head at the same time.

Christiane hung lots of spaghetti over her head, right in the middle of her long hair, and she said that now she was the **little mermaid**.

Mum couldn't stop laughing, especially at Uli, because he had tried to dive into the spaghetti with his head and got his face and hair full of sauce. She said we looked like

---

to look as though – so aussehen als ob
pigsty – Schweinestall
little mermaid – Kleine Meerjungfrau

monsters in a horror film and then Richard had the idea that we could play a frightening game after dinner.

It was a great idea and we stuffed the spaghetti down us as fast as possible so that we could start playing right away. We were all supposed to hide in our bedroom. One of us was the spaghetti monster who had to look for the others. The light was out so we couldn't see anything and we were afraid of the monster.

I was the birthday boy so I got first turn at being the monster. Everybody went into the bedroom and I waited in the corridor where I counted to a hundred slowly. I heard the grown-ups laughing in the living room and singing silly songs and I wondered why the grown-ups always had to have drinks to have fun.

Then I was finished counting.

I turned out the light in the hallway, **sneaked** into the playroom and closed the door behind me. I turned the key in the door and pulled it out so that nobody could escape. It was **pitch black**. I stood still for a moment and listened to see if I could hear anybody breathing. I could hear something ... but in the dark it was difficult to tell where it was coming from.

I took two steps forward and cried, here comes the spaghetti monster, I'm going to squash you all with the **roll-**

---

to sneak – schleichen, anschleichen
pitch black – stockfinster

ing pin and turn you into meat sauce! I made scary noises and ground my teeth.

I took a step forward and then I heard a strange sound, as though somebody was whimpering quietly right in front of me. It was really creepy and I got **goosebumps**. Hey, I said, stop that nonsense. I'm the spaghetti monster, I'm not afraid!

For a second there was absolute silence. Then something crashed into my face. I was so shocked I dropped the key to the door.

What had almost bashed in my nose was the door of our wardrobe. Susanne had been sitting inside crying with fear and then she shot out and pulled half of the clothes with her.

She groped around in the dark and suddenly she screamed that the spaghetti monster was here and had covered her in something cold and slippery.

Rubbish, said Christiane, that's my mermaid hair. Stop grabbing my face or I'll hit you!

But Susanne wasn't listening. She was still screaming and so Christiane slapped her across the face.

She was **right on target** because now Susanne screamed, my glasses, where are my glasses, I can't see any more! She felt her way around in the dark, crashing into the furniture and the walls. From the back of the room Dirk shouted, this is a stupid game, nobody can see any-

---

rolling pin – Nudelholz
goosebumps – Gänsehaut
to be right on target – einen Volltreffer landen

thing anyway and somebody should turn the light on before the silly blind cow bashes her head into something.

Stefan's voice called from somewhere up above that we couldn't put the light on because he'd taken the **bulb** out and then Bernd called out from up above as well, hey, watch what you're doing, you idiot!

Stefan said, idiot yourself, and Bernd smacked him and Stefan fell off the wardrobe where the two of them had been hiding.

The wardrobe is next to my bed, and so Stefan was lucky enough to fall into the blankets. Uli wasn't as lucky because he was *under* the blankets and it was worst of all for Dirk because he was under the bed and the bed collapsed under Stefan and Uli's weight.

Dirk started to shout for somebody to free him from the chaos and get Chubby Uli off him, and Uli **gasped** that he couldn't breathe.

And then Richard called out from the window, help is on the way, and there was **the sound of fabric tearing** and another crash.

Richard had been standing on the window sill behind the curtains and a screaming Susanne got there just as he was about to get down to help Dirk and Uli. Susanne crashed into him, Richard lost his balance and held on to

---

bulb – Glühbirne
to gasp – röcheln, nach Luft schnappen
the sound of fabric tearing – das Geräusch von zerreißendem Stoff

the curtain. The curtain ripped, Richard fell and knocked the brand new flower pot containing the remains of Mum's super-ivy off the window sill.

The flower pot fell on to the floor and broke, Richard fell on top of Susanne and everybody screamed all at once.

Bernd cried on top of the wardrobe that he didn't know how to get down and I **was afraid that** Dirk was injured and Uli was **suffocating** and I cried too and Christiane shouted, the door is closed, the door is closed, we're all going to die!

I crawled around on the floor feeling for the key but I couldn't find it. Instead Christiane stood on my left hand and tripped over me and slapped her spaghetti hair into my face.

Then Mum and Dad and the relatives banged against the door from the outside.

Mum screamed, oh God, oh God, the children, and Aunt Marianne screamed, Hiltrud, think of the baby, stay calm!

Uncle Alfred said we would have to break down the door and Aunt Erika yelled at him that he was so **dead drunk** that he couldn't even crack open a peanut. She sounded as though she had **put away** half of the drinks cabinet herself.

---

to be afraid that – befürchten, dass
to suffocate – ersticken
dead drunk – sturzbesoffen
to put away – *hier*: austrinken

Then I heard Dad tell us to move away from the door and make space. He gave a loud cry, there was a murderous crunch and suddenly it was light because Dad had kicked the door in and fallen into the room, right on top of Susanne's glasses. Later, when everybody had stopped crying and been collected by their parents and Dad and Mum had put all the drunk relatives into taxis and sent them home, Dirk and I lay in Dirk's bed, because mine was only good to be thrown away. Mum came in, sat down on the bed, and put an arm around both of us.

She said that we were the best boys in the world, but that we'd have to be a bit more careful in future, otherwise the baby would be born in the poor house with all the **damage** we were doing.

Then she gave us both a big kiss and said, go to sleep now, you two **rascals**, and left.

But Dirk and I stayed awake for a long time and when I fell asleep I dreamed of a spaghetti monster sitting drunk on a sledge with Fran in its lap and a bunch of flowers in its hand. The two of them were sliding down a giant buttercream cake between a thousand torches burning brightly and the monster kept on screaming, Andy Pandy, I wish you a very Happy Birthday!

---

damage – Zerstörung
rascal – Schlingel

Carrots in Space

The baby arrived in April.

The birth was very difficult for Mum and she was ill for quite a long time afterwards. Dad picked her and the baby up from the hospital. Dirk and I waited at home.

We had made a poster with the words: »Welcome from Dirk and Andreas!« We hung the poster over the door to the bedroom, because that's where the **cot** was.

When Mum and Dad came through the door, at first I was quite shocked because Mum was so **pale**. But she grinned and said, everything'll be fine and we should take a look at our new little brother.

Our new little brother was lying in a carry-cot, sleeping.

He was really tiny and pretty **ugly** too, I thought, but I didn't say that. Dad thought he was the most beautiful baby in the world, even though he had a bright red face and was all **scrumpled up**. He had a teeny weeny nose and his ears

---

cot – Babywiege, Gitterbett
pale – blass
ugly – hässlich
scrumpled up – verschrumpelt

were too big and stuck out from his head and overall his head looked like one of those bowls you serve soup from. He didn't have much hair either, and I felt sorry for him because he was so small and bald already. His hands were all wrinkled too.

And suddenly the baby opened his eyes. They were blue and slanted as though he came from China.

I thought, great, he'll recognise me right away.

But he didn't look at me at all, instead he opened his mouth and started to scream. His face got even redder and he waved his little arms around in the air. He didn't have a single tooth in his mouth.

No hair and no teeth, imagine that! And funny ears to top it all off!

Mum said, right, the baby's hungry.

She picked him up out of the cot, pulled up her jumper and pulled out one of her breasts. She attached the baby to it and he started to suck like mad and make grunting noises.

He sounded a bit like Fran and I said, we can call him Fran Two.

But the baby had a name already. He was called Björn and when he had finished sucking, he fell asleep again.

Pretty boring on the whole.

Ten weeks later Dirk and I lay under the blanket on my bed playing **starships**.

---

pretty boring on the whole – insgesamt total langweilig
starship – Raumschiff

That was our absolute favourite game. You had to crawl under the blanket until you reached the end of the bed, but with your head first. It was so dark under the bed that you could pretend you were in space. And of course you could see the sun and the earth and the moon, and the other planets flying around too. Then you got faster and raced through the **Milky Way**. Dirk and I **took turns** being the captain and the admiral and Fran was always an officer, but quite a bad one. We explored strange planets or fought against aliens. If the aliens were OK, then we made friends with them and had adventures together.

I had just blown up a giant meteorite that was about to ram into our ship when Dirk said the baby was boring. He was two months old and he did nothing except eat and sleep and cry. You couldn't play with him because he was too small. And he couldn't speak either.

And then he also said, he's stupid and he stinks!

I thought the baby was boring and stupid too, but the stinky thing wasn't fair. Babies can't go to the toilet because somehow **their bums don't work properly** yet. That's why they do it in their pants and you put nappies on them. We had discovered that it stank the most when Mum had fed the baby carrot puree. After that Dirk and I had sworn never to eat carrots again.

Milky Way – Milchstraße
to take turns – sich abwechseln
their bums don't work properly – ihre Hintern funktionieren nicht richtig

Because Dad was at work during the day and Mum was sick, Dirk and I did the housework. Mum had to lie in bed all day, apart from when the baby needed his nappy changing.

Dirk told her we could change the baby's nappy too. But Mum was afraid because Dirk always **drops** everything and you can't **mend** a baby. If it falls, then it might be broken for ever and you can't just hide it and get a new one.

But we were allowed to watch her changing nappies and even hold the baby's legs up.

Mum wiped his bottom. Then she washed, creamed and powdered it. But only his bottom. The baby was usually really quiet. Sometimes he waved his little fists in the air. He could even stick one foot in his mouth. Dirk and I tried it out, and we could do it too.

The baby's willy was really tiny and scrumpled. Once, he was lying on his back, all powdered and ready to go. Suddenly his willy went up and he weed without any warning. It went right into his left ear.

Dirk and I tried it out later but we didn't hit our ears. We made a real mess.

So we weren't allowed to change the baby's nappy, but we did everything else. We cooked and did the washing and tidied up and went shopping. Mum was really proud of

---

to drop something – etwas fallenlassen
to mend – *hier*: reparieren

us. We even prepared the food for the baby and sometimes we were even allowed to feed him. He could only eat **porridge** and mashed-up vegetables because he didn't have any teeth yet.

He was quite stupid! Dirk and I always ate biscuits in our spaceship, and Fran was allowed to eat the crumbs.

Dirk said, the baby would never be allowed in the spaceship because he was always spitting out his mashed-up vegetables and Fran wouldn't eat those. And apart from that we'd probably slip on the mush, then the ship wouldn't have a captain and we might crash into a planet.

I thought he was right. We were also a little bit afraid that the spaceship might stink of carrots.

The baby did have more hair now and Mum said he would have teeth soon. So there was hope after all, apart from the ears. But nonetheless we asked ourselves why a baby arrived when it wasn't even ready yet. It just made lots of work for other people. We had thought a little brother would be something quite different. We would rather not have had him or **exchanged** him for a new one.

All my friends looked at the baby.

Susanne thought he was great, of course. She was even allowed to hold him and she kept on saying coochy coochy coo and other stupid stuff. She probably thought he was

---

porridge – Brei
to exchange – eintauschen, umtauschen

great because his ears stuck out so much and because he'd probably have to wear braces when he was older just to top it all off.

Christiane thought the baby was OK, but Richard and Uli thought he was just as boring as Dirk and I. Well, said Richard, at least you can fall off a **skyscraper** with ears like that without anything happening to you. You'd sail right through the air like a glider.

Eventually Mum got better and she didn't have to lie in bed all day any more. And then came the day when Mum had to go to the doctor. Later, Mum told Dad it was a day she would never forget.

I'll never forget it either and neither will Dirk. That's because Dirk decided that the baby was old enough to become a spaceship admiral.

Mum had been at the doctor's for over two hours and I was standing in the kitchen heating **yukky** baby mush because it was almost feeding time. I was cross because I couldn't stand the stupid baby with his silly ears and all the rest. We would probably have to cook all kinds of things for him for years to come and as a **reward** all we'd get were stinky nappies.

Suddenly I heard the baby screaming.

I thought, great stuff, he's hungry right on time.

---

skyscraper – Wolkenkratzer
yukky – eklig
reward – Belohnung

Then Dirk screamed too and that's when I knew something had happened.

I raced into our bedroom and this is what I found: Dirk had taken the baby out of the cot and put him in his own bed. He had put Fran next to the baby, fetched a packet of biscuits, pulled a blanket over everything and started up the spaceship. He only wanted to go to the moon and at first everything was fine. Dirk ate biscuits, Fran ate the crumbs and the baby seemed to think everything was great too. But then, just before they landed on the moon, Dirk gave the baby a piece of biscuit. The baby **choked**, **coughed** and puked – bleuggh! – into the spaceship.

The entire bridge was covered in green vegetable mush and crumbs. Fran sat right in the middle. He had got half of the puke on him and he looked like an alien, green from top to bottom. He was grunting crossly. The baby was also full of mush and crumbs and I think he was angry too.

He screamed.

Dirk cried.

Fran grunted.

I swore.

The baby had filled his nappy from all the excitement. He stank of carrots and it was all a mess.

---

to choke – würgen
to cough – husten

I grabbed the baby, ran into the bathroom and put him on the **change table**.

He was still screaming. What a **racket**!

Dirk followed me. He looked shocked but he wasn't crying any more. I soaked a washcloth and wiped the baby's face. I sent Dirk back into our room to clean Fran and the sheets.

I wanted to change the baby's nappy, but I couldn't take it off properly because he was kicking and screaming. I was afraid he would fall, so I called Dirk back.

When he arrived, he was holding the bed sheets in one hand, and Fran in the other. He dropped both of them at the door. Happily, Fran landed on the sheets.

It was easier with two of us. We undressed the baby completely, which was hard work because he wouldn't keep still at all. And Fran was running around between our legs as well. The stupid sticky strip on the nappy wouldn't open at first, but we finally managed. Dirk was so beside himself that he threw the nappy into the toilet and flushed it. There was a glugging sound and then the toilet was **blocked** as well.

It was a good job that we had helped out with nappy changes before. I knew the order exactly: legs in the air, wipe, wash, oil, cream, powder. Unfortunately I used too

---

change table – Wickeltisch
racket – Lärm, Krawall
blocked – *hier*: verstopft
it was a good job that – *hier*: zum Glück

much oil and the cream wouldn't stick. So I put the rest of the cream on the baby's stomach. The baby thought that was great and finally stopped screaming. I tipped a lot of powder over everything to make sure everything was dry.

Dirk coughed. There was white powder everywhere.

And at that moment the baby decided to perform his **weeing-in-the-ear masterpiece**. So we had to start all over again because this time it didn't hit his ear but his **tummy** instead. It ran all down him, but he was in a very good mood and gurgled out of his toothless mouth.

I wanted to cry.

When we were finally finished, the baby looked really good. He only had a few crumbs in his ear.

I picked him up carefully and left the bathroom. The sheets were still on the floor and of course I stepped right into the vegetable puke. Suddenly there was a **burning smell**. The smell came from the kitchen, and there was lots of smoke because the porridge had boiled over.

Dirk ran into the kitchen. He almost stepped on Fran. Fran was still green. He was running wild through the flat and looked like a bowl of spinach on legs. I felt sick.

And then the front door opened.

Mum was back from the doctor's.

She sorted everything out.

---

weeing-in-the-ear masterpiece – Ins-Ohr-Pinkel-Kunststück
tummy – Bauch
burning smell – verbrannter Geruch

She fed the baby, got the nappy out of the blocked toilet and put the dirty sheets in the washing machine. I scrubbed the cooker and Dirk scrubbed Fran.

Mum wasn't cross with us, but she said **we really couldn't be trusted** to look after the baby by ourselves.

Then we both started to cry and she felt bad. The next day we bought a packet of our favourite cakes with our own pocket money and put them next to the baby in his cot. He looked at them a bit strangely, but then he laughed.

Mum thought that was great and she said, OK, you're big boys after all and in a few months the baby can fly through space with you.

So now, while he was being fed and having his nappy changed, we told the baby what it looked like in space and he seemed to really like us.

We called him Björn instead of Baby now. And it was really great having a little brother after all. We didn't want to **swap** him any more.

Well, maybe just his ears.

---

we really couldn't be trusted – man könne es uns nicht anvertrauen
to swap – eintauschen

The Plastic Bag

We would never have broken into the Bergers' **basement** if Richard hadn't got a telescope from his parents for his birthday.

Richard and his parents lived on the other side of the city. Richard's room was under the **roof** and he had a giant window above his bed. When you lay there, you could watch the stars in the sky and sometimes, when I was allowed to sleep over at Richard's, we imagined UFOs coming from outer space and flying with us to Vega or Orion. Richard knew all about stars and **constellations**, what they were called and why they shone and everything.

It's a little bit complicated cos usually several stars belong in a group. Whenever somebody thought, well, will you look at that, if you join that star with another one down there, it looks like a lion, then that became the lion constellation. And if, later on, somebody else thought,

---

basement – Keller
roof – Dach
constellation – *hier*: Sternbild

well, actually it looks more like an elephant or a **hoover**, there was nothing to be done, once a lion always a lion.

Richard once told me that the stars were so far away that sometimes their light dances through outer space for over a hundred years before it lands on earth. So a star could have exploded a long time ago, but we don't know that because its light still flies around for years until somebody suddenly notices that the lion doesn't have a tail any more, and even Richard doesn't know what happens then.

In any case, on the day when everything started, Susanne was at my house and we were doing our homework.

We were sitting at the table in the kitchen trying to find out how many legs run across a farmyard if seventeen pigs, fourteen chickens and nine cows live there, plus the farmer and his wife.

Dirk was watching us and getting on our nerves because he wanted to know why pigs don't lay eggs and cows only have one udder but four nipples to make up for it. Mum was standing at the sink doing the dishes when suddenly somebody hammered on the front door and the doorbell started to ring like mad.

Good grief, said Mum, who can that be, Björn will wake up from his lunchtime nap with all that noise. She went to the front door and opened it and Richard shot into

---

hoover – Staubsauger
good grief – meine Güte

the kitchen with a bright red face, out of breath and all excited.

He said he had something to tell us but it was a secret and he gave a sideways glance at Mum who was back at the sink.

Mum said the secret would have to wait until we'd figured out the thing with the legs in the farmyard.

Richard said, one hundred and thirty-six and could we go now. He was a clever one, Richard.

We went into the bedroom and sat on my bed, and Susanne, Dirk and I all had to swear that we would never tell anybody anything. Otherwise, Richard said, we would get **chicken pox**, mumps and measles all at once and diarrhoea too and then we would die slowly.

Susanne said she'd already had chicken pox and Richard said, OK, then she'd get the plague instead.

Susanne preferred to get the Russian flu because she'd read about it in the newspaper, and Dirk asked if he could have the plague instead of diarrhoea and Richard yelled that if we couldn't **make our minds up**, then we'd soon die of old age.

And then he finally told us his story.

The evening before he had been looking through his telescope again at the Bergers who lived in the last house on the other side of the street. There was a giant hedge

---

chicken pox – Windpocken
to make up one's mind – sich entscheiden

around the Bergers' garden, but because Richard's room was under the roof, he could see what was going on at the Bergers' quite easily from his window, especially with the telescope, even though his parents had banned him from looking in on them several times already.

And Richard had seen Mr and Mrs Berger **arguing** in their living room, where the light was on, and Mr Berger had **hit** his wife. Mrs Berger had run out of the living room, her husband had followed her and then the light had gone out.

Susanne said, men who hit women are pigs and machos.

Dirk asked what a macho was and Susanne thought about it and said, well, it must be something like the Russian flu, she'd read both things in the same newspaper anyway.

I asked Richard what the big secret was then, apart from the fact that Mr Berger hits his wife.

And then Richard said that he'd been bored earlier on while he was doing his homework and so he'd looked through the telescope. It was still **trained on** the Bergers' house from the evening before and he'd wanted to look at something else. But as he was looking through, he could see Mr Berger dragging a big black plastic **bin bag** from the living room out of the patio door across the patio and through the garden over to a door that led down into the

---

to argue – streiten
to hit – schlagen
to be trained on something – auf etwas gerichtet sein
bin bag – Müllsack

cellar. He pulled the bag in there, sweating like crazy. Luzy, the Bergers' sheepdog, had howled the whole time and tried to scratch at the plastic. Then Mr Berger came out of the cellar again with Luzy but without the bag and went back into the house.

Richard ran into the kitchen, took a few eggs out of the fridge and went over to the Bergers. He rang the doorbell.

Mr Berger opened the door and Richard nearly died of fear. But he said that these were the eggs that his mother had borrowed from Mrs Berger and he wanted to give them back and was Mrs Berger at home. And Mr Berger was really unfriendly and said his wife had gone away and that he was going away soon as well and then Richard gave him the eggs and ran away and jumped on to his bike and came over to us and that was that.

I thought it was really creepy and I said, **crikey**, and Dirk said, that's unbelievable, and Susanne said, what, I don't get it.

Richard rolled his eyes and whispered, wasn't it **obvious**: Mr Berger had killed his wife, wrapped her body in a plastic bag and hidden it in the cellar.

Susanne's eyes opened wide behind her thick glasses.

Dirk whispered, Mr Berger had probably strungled his wife. Richard said it was **strangled** and that wasn't neces-

---

crikey – *Ausruf*: o Mann
obvious – offensichtlich
to strangle someone – jemanden erwürgen

sarily what had happened, and Dirk said, exactly, maybe he'd just **stubbed** her, in any case she was as **dead as a dodo** now and all wrapped up.

For a moment we were all quiet, looking at each other.

Dirk said, nobody'll believe us, and I said, what will we do now, and then Susanne whispered, yes, what we will do now, because if Mrs Berger is all killed and Mr Berger has gone away, who's going to feed poor Luzy?

Richard looked at Susanne as though she wasn't all there and then he looked at Dirk and me and I knew what he was going to say because I had the same idea.

We can't go to the police, said Richard, because they don't listen to children. So we have to **prove** that Mr Berger is a murderer ourselves. And to prove that, we would have to get into the Bergers' cellar somehow and find the plastic bag with the body.

That evening we all went over to Richard's.

We had told our parents that it was a special evening because there were tons of **shooting stars** that we wanted to watch through the telescope. Richard's parents were having dinner with some friends and were supposed to come back at ten o'clock and then Richard's dad would drive us home. So everything was set for us to break into the cellar.

---

stubbed – *Wortschöpfung aus*: to stab someone – jemanden erstechen; to stub out something – etwas ausdrücken

dead as a dodo – mausetot

to prove – beweisen

shooting stars – Sternschnuppen

We had all put on our darkest clothes and Dirk had brought his small torch. At eight o'clock it was already completely dark outside and I was so excited that I had to go to the loo twice.

Richard painted our faces black with **soot** from a singed cork and we all looked great, like proper burglars, I thought.

Susanne was carrying a small rucksack and said she was **petrified**. What would happen, for example, if Luzy caught us, or Mr Berger, and he wrapped us *all* up in plastic bags.

Richard said Luzy was so stupid that she couldn't tell a bone from a phone. She wouldn't harm us. And if Mr Berger did us in, then we would have died for **justice** and would go to heaven like angels – even though it would be difficult to fly around in a plastic bag and play an instrument at the same time and sing Jesus songs.

Then he looked at us all happily and said now we would have to swear that we would either find Mrs Berger's body and deliver her murderer to the police or die doing it. Dirk said, all right then, and off we went.

It started off well. We had run out of the house and over the street without anybody seeing us and then around the Bergers' house until we were at the back next to their hedge. We had to climb through it. It was so dark that we

---

soot – Ruß
petrified – *hier*: versteinert (vor Schreck)
justice – Gerechtigkeit

could barely see a thing and if I hadn't known that the others were standing next to me, I really wouldn't have seen them because our **camouflage** was so good.

Richard was the first to creep into the hedge, Dirk was next and then me and Susanne last. We made quite a loud rustling and the branches scratched our faces. And because it had rained, drops of water fell down the back of my anorak.

Richard, Dirk and I were already lying on the lawn on the other side of the hedge, hiding, when Susanne suddenly started swearing that **she was stuck** because her stupid rucksack had got caught in the branches. She started jumping around in the hedge like a lunatic and made an awful lot of noise.

Richard hissed, be quiet and what's in the stupid rucksack anyway.

Susanne stopped hopping around and called back, stupid question, something to eat and drink of course, the cup for her braces and three Mickey Mouse comics in case Mr Berger caught us and locked us up.

He'll almost certainly do that, Richard whispered back, if Susanne carries on being so stupid with her jumping around and shouting!

Then Dirk shouted to Susanne, why hadn't she brought the Marsupilami comics instead of Mickey Mouse or at the

---

camouflage – Tarnung
to be stuck – festsitzen, festklemmen

very least the **Smurfs**, and Richard yelled at him, he would whack him over the head if he didn't shut his mouth right away, and at that moment Susanne crashed through the hedge and fell on to the wet grass next to Dirk.

It was so loud that I thought Mr Berger would hear it and we all stayed on the grass not daring to breathe.

But Mr Berger hadn't heard anything. We could see him through the living room window from where we lay on the grass. He was sitting in front of the television with a bottle of beer in his hand, and Luzy was lying in front of his chair on the carpet, sleeping.

Richard whispered that we should keep our heads down and follow him, and then he crawled over the lawn towards the cellar door. We crept behind him and once I put my hand on something slimy, a **snail** that was crawling around. That was really **disgusting**.

Richard reached the cellar door first, then Susanne and I arrived and then Dirk suddenly hurtled across, nose to the ground, shot past us and crashed headfirst into the wall of the house at top speed.

Richard said he must be crazy and Dirk nearly **burst into tears** and rubbed his head and said that Richard should try crawling around with his head on the ground not seeing anything and that he really needed a wee.

---

smurf – Schlumpf
snail – Schnecke
disgusting – ekelhaft
to burst into tears – in Tränen ausbrechen

Richard didn't answer because he was already trying to open the cellar door. The door was locked of course but there was a small, half-open window in the wall right next to it.

Richard whispered, we have to go in there, Susanne first because she might get stuck again and then it would be easier to push her in from the outside than to pull her down from the inside. The cellar was probably quite far down and we might not be able to reach Susanne from the inside.

Susanne said, Richard must **have a screw loose**, she wasn't going into the cellar by herself with a body down there in plastic, with no light or anything. And if the cellar was that deep, she could break all her bones and maybe Mrs Berger was in there just waiting for small children to fall into the cellar so she could eat them all up.

I said, that's rubbish, dead people don't run around like that, and definitely not in the dark wrapped in plastic because that would be even more difficult than competing in a sack race.

Susanne took a deep breath and said, all right then, she would go in first – but only to prove that girls were braver than boys.

Then she pushed open the window, pulled herself through the frame, wiggled her legs for a minute, kicked me in the stomach with one foot and **disappeared**.

---

to have a screw loose – eine Schraube locker haben, eine Meise haben
to disappear – verschwinden

We heard a soft landing and then Susanne called up from inside that she was fine and that there was a washing basket under the window and that she had fallen into it. Dirk should pass her the torch through the window so that she could look for her glasses which had fallen into the washing somewhere.

Dirk passed his torch down to Susanne and climbed in after it. There was another landing noise and Dirk was inside. Then it was my turn and it was really exciting landing in the soft washing even though it was quite stinky because I had landed in some of Mr Berger's pongy socks. I climbed out of the basket and Richard was already tumbling through the window.

Susanne had found her glasses again. She was standing in front of the washing basket, shining the torch on us, saying that the basket would be great for our **escape**. We only had to put the lid on, then we could climb back up out of the window.

Up until now everything had happened so quickly that I hadn't had any time to be afraid. But suddenly I found everything really **scary** because Susanne's voice sounded all strange in the basement, and then nobody said anything any more and that was even scarier. I **pictured** poor Mrs Berger in her plastic bag. She was probably scared out of

---

escape – Flucht
scary – furchterregend
to picture something – sich etwas vorstellen

her wits as well, what with spending all night in the dark dead and all.

The basement was pretty small. It smelled of the clothes from the basket and of washing powder and it was completely dark because Dirk's torch wasn't all that strong. We didn't dare to put on the light in case Mr Berger saw light coming from the basement window if he happened to look out of his living room into the garden.

I held on tight to Dirk and we went over to Richard and Susanne who were standing behind us. The few steps we took click-clacked and made little echos and I got goosebumps everywhere. Susanne pointed the torch at one wall and in the beam of light we saw a door that probably led upstairs. Next to it there was a washing machine and a **tumble dryer**. On the next wall there was a shelf crammed full of jam jars and on the wall next to that lots of garden tools hung on lots of little hooks. The last wall was the one with the door that led into the garden and the window with the washing basket underneath it.

And right there, next to the washing basket, lay the plastic bag.

For a while we stood in front of it and looked at the plastic shining in the light from the torch.

Richard **swallowed** and whispered that now we would have to open the bag.

---

tumble dryer – Wäschetrockner
to swallow – schlucken

Susanne said that she really didn't want to see a proper dead body.

Dirk said, exactly, who knows what it looks like, all strungled and everything, and that Mrs Berger might even still have her eyes open and look all strange and that maybe she was quite comfortable in her plastic bag and would be cross if we opened it.

Richard said there was no way out of it, we had to open the bag because otherwise we wouldn't have any **proof** for the police. He pulled his **penknife** out of his right trouser pocket and said, come on then.

Susanne gave Dirk the torch and said he should shine the light because she was too afraid.

Dirk started to shake holding the torch and my legs shook too. Susanne took a few steps back and Richard cut the plastic with his torch and ripped it open.

At first nothing happened. But then Richard pulled at the plastic and something rustled and fell out of the bag and on to the floor with a crash.

Susanne jumped back and screamed, that's Mrs Berger's cut-off hand, the macho has cut her into pieces!

As she did so she brushed against one of the jam jars on the shelf behind her and it fell. Susanne **groped at** the glass and even managed to catch it, but she crashed against

---

proof – Beweis
penknife – Taschenmesser
to grope at something – nach etwas greifen

the shelf with full force. The shelf wobbled and rattled and a whole lot of glasses fell off and they made such a loud noise as they crashed on to the floor that it sounded as though an aeroplane was landing in the cellar.

Susanne screamed.

Dirk screamed too and then the idiot went and dropped his torch and it was pitch black.

I started to scream too because now the plastic was rustling really loudly and Susanne screamed, oh God, oh God, now she's coming to eat us! Dirk started to cry that he was afraid and couldn't hold his wee any longer and we all ran around in the dark screaming at the top of our voices.

I crashed hard into a wall and saw lots of bright lights, turned around in a circle, took a few steps, **tripped** over something and fell into the washing basket, right into the pongy socks.

Richard shouted that we should stop screaming, there wasn't anybody in the plastic bag, there was only washing in there, but I didn't care. Susanne and Dirk were also still screaming and I was trying really hard to pull the **lid** of the washing basket over me when the door to the cellar flew open and the light went on.

At first I couldn't see anything because it was suddenly really light but after two or three seconds I recognised Mr

---

to trip – stolpern
lid – Deckel

Berger. He was standing in the door with a proper pistol in his hand shouting, put your hands up you swine, otherwise I'll blow your brains out!

Susanne said, crap, it's macho man, and we all put our hands up and the lid on the washing basket crashed on to my head. There was a loud bang and I was **terrified to death** because I thought Mr Berger had shot one of us. But it was only the jam jar that Susanne had caught earlier on but had now dropped.

The next moment Luzy **shot down** the stairs behind Mr Berger like lightning. She pushed past him to the plastic bag and grabbed the thing that had fallen out. And then she placed it in the middle of the basement and wagged her tail.

Boy, were we in trouble!

Mr Berger was really angry and **grassed on us** of course, the idiot. Richard had his telescope confiscated for two weeks by his parents and Mum and Dad were really cross because Dirk and I had lied to them about the shooting stars, and Susanne's parents were cross too. It was all really embarrassing. There had only been washing in the plastic bag. And the reason Luzy had gone crazy was because Mr Berger had wrapped her favourite bone in there by mistake. It had fallen out when Richard cut open the

---

terrified to death – zu Tode erschrocken
to shoot down – *hier*: herunterrasen
to grass on someone – jemanden verpetzen

bag. And Mrs Berger really was on holiday after all and altogether we felt really stupid.

Although, Richard said two weeks later when he was allowed to use his telescope again and Dirk, Susanne and I visited him, grown-ups are really the stupid ones! Instead of being happy that children **keep an eye on them** so they don't kill each other, they pretend **everything is hunky dory** and everybody gets along with everybody else just fine. Whereas really they're macho men and go around hitting each other!

Dirk said, exactly, and in future I couldn't care less whether the grown-ups **bump each other off** because whether they stub or strungle each other, they're only a bit quicker than the Russian flu or old age.

---

to keep an eye on someone – auf jemanden aufpassen
everything is hunky dory – alles ist in Butter
to bump each other off – sich gegenseitig abmurksen

Persians and Pomegrenades

There was snow outside again. A year had passed since we had visited the old people's home and then, a few weeks before the Christmas holidays, a new boy joined our class. And because Richard had flu, he missed it all.

Miss Weide, our teacher, told us a few days beforehand that we were getting a new classmate and that he was a **Persian** and his name was Bearuss.

Jörg said, my mum has a Persian too, it's in our living room and we call it the eye of the Orient.

At first I thought Jörg was **having us on**, but then Miss Weide explained to us that Jörg's mother's Persian was a **carpet**.

Apparently there are lots of different kinds of carpets in the world and if they come from Persia, then they're called Persians. Persia is quite a far-off country somewhere next to Africa. It used to be called Persia and now it's called Iran. They have a lot of desert, oil, **pomegre-**

Persian – Perser
to have someone on – jemanden veräppeln
carpet – Teppich

nades and carpets in Iran and the carpets are really expensive because they have a lot of knots. And the people who live in Persia are called Persians too, just like the carpets but without knots. A bit like a Hamburger. If Hamburgers come from Hamburg, then they're people, but if they come from McDonald's, they're a hundred per cent **beef**.

We were really excited about the new boy. He arrived on a Monday just as we were doing maths. There was a knock on the door and then it opened and the headmaster, Mr Bartel, came in.

Mr Bartel was the smallest grown-up I knew. He had hairs in only a few places on his head and he combed them in all directions so that it looked as though he had more. He had a funny way of talking as well and he had bad breath. But you only noticed that when he looked you straight in the eye and said, well, dear Andreas, have we forgotten to do our homework again?

Mr Bartel came in and said, children, you're getting a new boy in your class, behave yourselves and be nice to him. He went outside into the corridor and said, well, Bearuss, come on in, and Bearuss came in and Mr Bartel closed the door from the outside.

Miss Weide led Bearuss right up to the board so that we could all see him. He was as tall as I was and he had curly

---

pomegrenade – *Wortschöpfung aus*: pomegranate – Granatapfel; grenade – Granate
beef – Rindfleisch

black hair, really brown skin and brown eyes and was quite fat. Everybody started whispering. Miss Weide called out, quiet please, Bearuss is going to **introduce himself**.

We were all very surprised because he spoke German really well!

He said, my name is Bearuss, that's spelled B-E-H-R-U-Z and in Persian it means most beautiful day. Then he said that he had gone to a German school in Persia because his mother actually came from Austria and that he liked to eat **sunflower seeds** and when he was bigger he was going to be a government minister.

Chubby Uli started to laugh and said, of course, and when *he* grew up he was going to be Chancellor and eat nothing but **bird seed**.

Uli was actually really nice but sometimes he was stupid too and a show-off. He didn't want to be Chancellor at all. He wanted to be a dancer and he took proper ballet lessons. In **P.E**. he sometimes ran through the gym making funny movements and shaking his bottom. Once, when he tried to spin round on tiptoe really quickly, he had fallen on to his nose quite badly and broken one of his top teeth.

Anyway, Behruz looked at him and said, if you make

---

to introduce oneself – sich (mit Namen) vorstellen
sunflower seeds – Sonnenblumenkerne
bird seed – Vogelfutter
P.E. – *kurz für*: Physical Education – Sportunterricht

fun of me, there'll be a price to pay, **let's get that straight**, and we all started laughing, apart from Uli.

Miss Weide cried out, children, let's not start fighting, and fingered her pearl necklace nervously. Miss Weide was always really nervous and was afraid that we would get into fights and that terrible things would happen, and then she needed her necklace because of all the excitement.

She told Behruz to write his name on the board in Persian.

It looked great the way Behruz wrote it, with flourishes and little lines that weren't proper letters but you could still read them. After that Miss Weide wanted to put Behruz in Christiane's seat next to Susanne. Christiane was at home in bed with flu like Richard and that's why her seat was empty.

And that's where the trouble started.

Behruz looked at Susanne and said he would never sit next to a girl and he'd get spots if he did because women were stupid.

Susanne was insulted and **hissed back**, fine, I don't want to sit next to a spotty macho who chews sunflower seeds all day either.

Behruz growled at her, I'll smack you so hard in a minute that your braces will fly off your teeth, and Susanne shouted back, just try it, you big mouth, then I'll knock your teeth in and shove pomegranades up your nose.

---

let's get that straight – damit das klar ist
to hiss back – zurückfauchen

Miss Weide almost put a knot in her pearl necklace out of **sheer desperation**. You could **hear a pin drop** in the classroom.

But Behruz looked at Susanne and said she was great. Because Persians were the bravest people in the world and that's why he thought brave girls were fantastic, especially when they were as pretty as Susanne. And they weren't pomegrenades but pomegranates, and he would bring her some one day.

Then he sat down next to her and shook her hand and I bet Susanne fell in love with him on the spot because of his big brown eyes. She didn't say another word and went bright red.

Miss Weide was really **relieved** that there hadn't been a fight. She said, well, now we can carry on with the lesson.

Nothing happened in the lesson. But everybody looked **curiously** over at Behruz who was copying down the sums from the board as though he'd been in our class forever and really did belong there.

The next day Miss Weide had an accident in her old VW Beetle.

The streets were really slippy that morning with black ice, because the snow had melted a bit the previous day and

---

sheer desperation – pure Verzweiflung
to hear a pin drop – eine Stecknadel fallen hören; *hier*: es wurde mucksmäuschenstill
relieved – erleichtert
curiously – neugierig

had frozen again at night. That's why Miss Weide couldn't brake in her **old banger** when she was driving down the hill. She skidded at full speed over the main street into Gelbecke's butcher's, right through the front window that reached all the way down to the pavement.

The Beetle destroyed the **spice rack** and the microwave oven and crashed into the counter and there were shards of glass everywhere.

Mrs Gelbecke told us later on that it was lucky there hadn't been any customers in the shop and the only thing that had happened was that the little advent wreath had fallen off the counter into the pork goulash and a few jars of mayonnaise had smashed. It had actually been quite funny, Mrs Gelbecke said, because she saw Miss Weide let go of the steering wheel, scream like mad and reach for her pearl necklace even before she came through the window.

Miss Weide wasn't hurt because she had been wearing her seatbelt, but she was in shock. She got out of the car, went to the counter where Mrs Gelbecke was standing, completely **stupefied**, and tried to buy half a pig to give to her sister at Christmas. Could Mrs Gelbecke please wrap it up nicely, in shiny paper and with a **ribbon** and so on and add a few sausages to the package so that her sister wouldn't think she couldn't afford a proper present?

---

old banger – *umgangssprachlich*: Klapperkiste
spice rack – Gewürzregal
stupefied – verschreckt
ribbon – Band, Geschenkband

Then her necklace ripped and the pearls rolled all over the floor of the butcher's shop.

Anyway, because of the shock Miss Weide couldn't come to school.

So that morning Mr Bartel came into the classroom and said, children, take out your books and be quiet. Mrs Zenker will be here for the next class, so behave yourselves until then.

Mr Bartel had only just left the room when Uli stood up.

He called out, hey, Persian, and it went very quiet in the classroom.

Behruz looked at Uli, who was walking over to him like a cowboy going into a bar in a Western. I thought, now there'll be a fight. But Uli stood in front of Behruz and said, if you're really as brave as you say you are and not just a big mouth, how about a little test of your courage, Mr Government Minister?

Behruz said, no problem, Mr Chancellor, what's it to be?

Uli grinned and said that Behruz should climb out of one of the two big windows in our classroom and walk outside along the **window ledge** to the next window.

Everybody gasped.

First of all, our classroom is on the fourth floor of the school and there were at least twelve metres between us and the playground below. Secondly, the windows were set out in such a way that Behruz would have to go round a

---

window ledge – Fenstersims

corner to get from one window to another. Thirdly, there was snow on the window ledge. Fourthly, the window ledge was really narrow, about twenty centimetres wide. And fifthly, it was snowing like mad and it was really windy.

Anyway, the first thing would have been enough to stop me climbing out of the window and I don't think Behruz was all that **keen** either.

Susanne said to Uli that she thought it was a great idea and maybe he could go first. She would wipe up the fat stain from where Uli smacked into the school playground. And if he and Behruz went ahead and did it, then they were macho men and stupid show-offs and tired of life.

But Uli didn't listen to Susanne. He looked at Behruz and Behruz looked at Uli and it was still just like a Western.

And then Behruz said, OK, **lardy arse**, but if I manage it, it's your turn next.

The line about the lardy arse was great, I thought, even though Behruz was just as fat as Uli. And Behruz's idea was great too. Uli went all pale and I thought, he'll **chicken out** and then Behruz won't have to climb out on to the window ledge and everything will be OK and we can eat sunflower seeds together.

But instead Uli said, it's a deal, you **seed chomper**, so off you go.

---

to be keen on something – auf etwas scharf sein, Lust auf etwas haben
lardy arse – Fettsack, *hier*: Speckwalze
to chicken out – sich drücken
seed chomper – Körnerfresser

And Behruz stood up and I had a funny feeling in my stomach, as though a school of fish were swimming round in there. Nobody said anything when he opened the window and climbed on to a chair and got out on to the window ledge.

And because everybody was watching Behruz, nobody noticed Susanne creeping out of the classroom.

Thank God his shoes weren't slippy. Behruz took a few steps to the right until he was up against the wall with no window behind him. The whole class pushed forward and squashed up together because everybody wanted to see what was going on. Uli stood right at the front and looked at Behruz and bit his lip.

By then I thought the whole test of courage thing was pretty stupid and I was afraid that Behruz would fall. Then he'd be dead and we'd be **guilty** because nobody had stopped him and his parents would be cross because he wouldn't become a government minister.

I felt really sick.

Behruz had almost reached the corner where he had to go around the wall. He had pressed his back and his arms against the wall and was taking little sideways steps, pushing the snow off the ledge because he wasn't picking his feet up. He looked straight ahead and didn't look down once.

If he *had* looked down he would have seen Mr Bartel standing down in the playground with Susanne next to

---

guilty – schuldig

him. Snowflakes were blowing around the two of them and Mr Bartel's hair flew around his head in all directions.

He shouted up, young man, get off the ledge and back into the classroom **immediately**! Susanne shouted something too but you couldn't hear it properly.

Behruz stood still.

And I could see him crying through the snowflakes that were blowing around him.

That's the way it goes: first you're brave and as long as you're not afraid, everything is fine. And then suddenly you *are* afraid and you can't move. And when you're twelve metres above the ground on a window ledge, then you're really **in a mess**.

Uli could see Behruz crying and Mr Bartel **leaping around** down in the playground and Susanne who was crying now too.

Somebody asked, what should we do now?

Uli took a deep breath and said, well, because the whole mess was his fault, he would go and bring Behruz back. And suddenly he was standing on the window ledge.

Mr Bartel was screeching like Granny when she is having one of her heart attacks. Maybe he thought that the rest of the class was going to climb out too. In any case, he ran back into the building.

---

immediately – sofort
to be in a mess – in der Tinte sitzen
to leap around – herumspringen

Susanne's voice squeaked up that Mr Bartel had gone to get the fire brigade.

Crikey, this was the most exciting thing I'd ever seen and I was annoyed that Dirk and Richard weren't there. Now other teachers came out into the playground and there were children looking out of all the windows. Everybody was screaming and then the door of the classroom Mr Holm, our sports teacher, ran in.

He yelled that we must have all gone crazy and he ran to the open window where tons of snowflakes were flying in.

He leaned out and shouted at Uli and Behruz not to move.

He didn't need to say it, because **in the meantime** Uli was standing next to Behruz, crying. They were holding tightly on to each other's hand and I could see Uli's legs shaking.

They stood like that for at least five minutes while Mr Holm told them they had to be brave and help was on the way. Mr Bartel was back out in the playground running up and down in between the other teachers and Susanne was running up and down after Mr Bartel and there was absolute chaos.

Then we heard the siren of the fire engine getting louder and louder and then everything happened really quickly. The fire engine skidded over the playground with its lights flashing and lots of firemen jumped out. Some of

---

in the meantime – währenddessen

them spread out a giant **rescue net** right under Behruz and Uli and others began putting up their ladder.

I thought, thank God, because I was afraid that Behruz and Uli would freeze out there on the ledge because it was so cold and then they would get covered in snow. I looked over at the two of them. They were still holding hands and shivering.

And suddenly both of them stopped shivering. Behruz looked down at the rescue net. Uli also looked down at the rescue net. And I saw the two of them grinning at each other.

I think I screamed, just as everybody else did, when Behruz and Uli closed their eyes and jumped off the window ledge down into the whirling snowflakes.

The next day Behruz and Uli weren't in school because they both had colds. But their parents had to go and see Mr Bartel and be told how stupid their sons were. In the fourth lesson Mr Bartel came into our class and was really cross. Miss Weide was back and while Mr Bartel was **telling us off**, she didn't know what to do with her hands because her pearl necklace had snapped in the butcher's shop and she hadn't had time to buy a new one.

Mr Bartel said that he didn't think all that much of us for **going along with** all the nonsense. He said, I didn't

---

rescue net – Sprungtuch
to tell someone off – jemanden ausschimpfen
to go along with something – bei etwas mitmachen

become headmaster to end up in a **mental hospital** because of some idiots. And he said, sometimes it's much braver to say no instead of proving how great you are by climbing buildings and jumping into rescue nets.

I could see that Mr Bartel was right.

But I still thought it was really brave of them to jump into the rescue net and I said that to Behruz when I visited him that afternoon with Susanne.

We had only been there for five minutes and we were sitting on Behruz's bed where he was covered in at least ten blankets when the door bell rang.

Uli was standing outside and asked if he could come in. He had a big scarf around his neck and looked as though he'd been crying a lot because he'd been in trouble with his parents. He had a bag of sunflower seeds in one hand and in the other a pomegranate.

We ate everything up and drank Persian tea and laughed a lot when Behruz and Uli took turns telling us what it felt like to fly through the air with snow all around them and how they had almost **wet their pants with fear**. And I thought it was typical that two boys who couldn't stand each other at first were now great friends.

Really great friends.

---

mental hospital – Irrenhaus
to wet one's pants with fear – sich vor Angst in die Hose machen

Pigs, Ladders, Cement Mixers

The following summer an aunt of dad's died and left him a house in town. The house had been standing empty for a long time because the aunt had lived somewhere else.

Dad told us he couldn't stand his aunt and she couldn't stand him either. That's why he'd never visited her. She had almost certainly only left him the house because she could stand the other members of Dad's family even less.

Anyway, Mum and Dad had decided to renovate the house and move in, and one weekend in June we all got into the car and drove to see Dad's **inheritance**.

Our new house was almost at the end of the street and it was the ugliest house I had ever seen. But I recognised it again immediately, because two weeks beforehand Dirk and I had smashed in almost all the **window panes** with a catapult. I didn't feel bad doing it because the house was all **run down** anyway, a proper ruin. The **plaster was crumbling**

---

inheritance – Erbschaft
window panes – Fensterscheibe
run down – heruntergekommen
the plaster was crumbling – der Putz fiel herab

everywhere and there were **tiles** lying around that had fallen off the roof.

Dad grinned and was very proud. He said, well, this is our new home and what did we think of it. I thought it was stupid but I didn't say anything.

Then we all went inside and stood around in the hallway and Mum said, the place looks like it's been hit by a bomb.

I didn't know why anybody would want to set a bomb off in our new house, but it must have a big one! Everything was broken and dirty inside. There were bits of wallpaper and spiders' webs hanging from the walls. It smelt really **mouldy**, the way it did in Fran's pen the time he'd eaten green **play-doh** and had got diarrhoea from it.

On the ground floor there were three rooms and a kitchen and a bathroom as well as the hallway. There was stuff everywhere. Dirk and I would have liked to look through everything, but we weren't allowed.

I thought it was strange that Dad spent the whole time grinning but he obviously wasn't afraid that the ceiling would fall on his head like I was.

Dirk thought it was all great. He said that the spiders' webs and the dust and the creaking of the floor made it like Sleeping Beauty's castle after her hundred-year sleep.

---

tile – Dachziegel
mouldy – vermodert, muffig
play-doh – Knete

Mum thought he was right because nobody appeared to have cleaned in here for at least a hundred years.

Rickety stairs led up to the top floor. They were so rotten that you couldn't balance properly. Dad went first, followed by Mum with Björn in her arms and then Dirk.

I stayed where I was because I wanted to wait and see if the staircase collapsed. Then I would have been an **orphan** with nothing, just the stupid house, and I probably would have **starved**. Or Uncle Alfred would have adopted me. Or Aunt Gertrud. Or maybe Aunt Marianne. In any case, I would rather have starved.

But nothing happened when everybody stomped up the stairs, so I followed them.

Upstairs there was even more dirt and mess than there was downstairs, but Dad went on grinning.

Mum said the house was one big rubbish bin, and it would be better **to pull it down** and build a new one.

She had put Björn down on the ground and it only took him ten seconds to cover himself in dirt.

Mum quickly picked him up again and said to Dad, fabulous, the kid has just picked up more **germs** than Europe during the plague! I think Dad's constant grin was getting on her nerves.

---

orphan – Waise
to starve – verhungern
to pull something down – etwas abreißen
germs – Keime

There were four rooms and Dad said, well, we will knock that wall through, then we'll have a big living room, and the other two rooms are for Dirk and Andreas.

He ran up and down as though he was measuring everything out with his arms. He knocked against the plaster on the wall that was going to be knocked through. **That'll be a tough one**, he said, it's very well built.

He knocked against the wall again and it crumbled and Dad didn't grin any more but looked thoughtful instead. When he banged against the wall a third time, he made a big hole in it, as big as a door. There was a loud noise and all kinds of stones fell on to the floor.

I thought, now everything will collapse and I wished I'd stayed downstairs. But there was just a thick cloud of dust.

Dad said, it's not as bad as it looks, and laughed.

Mum pursed her lips in a strange way.

We went back downstairs again. Dirk gave a cry like Tarzan and jumped the last stairs down to the hallway. He shouldn't have done that. There was a bit of a crunch and then he broke though the floor with both of his feet at the same time. It wasn't a deep hole and Dirk wasn't stuck, but he cried all the same.

Mum said the whole house was a **bloody death trap**! Dad just wanted **to cash in on her life insurance** and **he**

---

that'll be a tough one – das wird schwierig
bloody death trap – verdammte Todesfalle
to cash in on one's life insurance – die Lebensversicherung ausbezahlt bekommen

shouldn't convince himself that it would be easy to raise three sons without their mother.

But Dad said, you shouldn't look a gift horse in the mouth, and I thought, great, we're getting a horse too!

Mum explained to me later that it was a saying.

The gift was the house, and because it was free we couldn't grumble. It would be like being given a horse with no teeth, you couldn't grumble then either. I knew what Granny looked like without her teeth, and I felt really sorry for the horse.

We couldn't get into the basement from above, because the neighbour who had looked after the house, Mr Grau, kept his pigs in there.

Mum said, absolutely nobody is opening the hallway door to the basement. It's bad enough that it looks like a pigsty in here, it doesn't need to stink like one too!

So we went through the garden instead. There was another door on the outside and that led into the basement.

The first room was very large and most of it was taken up by the pigsty, which had a fence all around it. There were five pigs in there, all of them pink and still quite small with **curly tails** and all the rest.

Mum and Dad looked around. Dad said, what a mess, the basement floor needs re-concreting as soon as the pigs are out of here.

---

he shouldn't convince himself that – er solle nicht glauben, dass
curly tail – Ringelschwanz

Then he went into the next room with Mum.

Dirk and I looked at the pigs. Dirk rumpled up his nose. They really did stink quite badly and they were pretty dirty too, but I thought they were OK and Björn did too.

The pigs were really great but I don't think they were that smart. When I lifted Björn up over the fence and sat him on the back of one so that he could have a ride, they raced up and down the pigsty in excitement. Björn fell off the pig and right into the dirt because he hadn't held on tightly enough to the pig's ears. The pig ran over to its friends who were all squeezed into one corner.

Björn crawled over to them, from one pile of dirt to another, and they must have thought he was one of them. One of them was really brave. It went up to Björn and sniffed at him.

Björn said didi dada and stuck a finger into its snout.

Quick as a flash **all hell broke loose** because the pig squealed really loudly and ran over to the others, and then Mum and Dad came back and saw Björn in the pig's dirt and screamed, and Dirk and I screamed too, and Björn started to cry and there was one hell of a racket.

Dad jumped over the fence as though he was in a **murder mystery**, but he landed in the middle of a pile of poo, slipped and fell into the dirt. The pigs rushed out of their corner squealing.

---

all hell broke loose – die Hölle brach los, der Teufel war los
murder mystery – Krimi

I thought, great, now there'll be a mud fight! But Dad picked himself up and grabbed Björn with one arm and was back out in a flash.

Mum shouted at the pigs that she would personally make sausages out of them all and out of the stupid neighbour too.

Then she **hugged** Björn and Dad, and Dirk and I were the only ones who didn't have pig dirt sticking to us.

A few weeks later everything looked very different.

All the rubbish had been cleared away. We had thrown everything that was upstairs out of the windows into the garden. It was all put into a **trailer** and taken to the **rubbish dump**.

We had put down a new floor and put in new wiring because there wasn't enough electricity. New windows and heating were put in and everything was new in the bathroom too.

We couldn't move in yet because the wallpaper had to go up first. The basement wasn't ready yet either because the pigs were still living down there. But Mr Grau had finally found somewhere else for them to live. **They were supposed to** be moving to a farmyard.

Dirk and I wanted to keep one of them so we could

---

to hug – umarmen
trailer – *hier*: Anhänger
rubbish dump – Müllkippe
they were supposed to – sie sollten

teach Björn how to ride and so that Fran would have somebody to play with.

But Mum said, not a single one of those stupid pigs is staying in this house! It would be too dangerous for Björn and Fran because both of them could be trampled on. And she had no desire to spend the rest of her life in a house that stank of pigs and apart from that we needed the basement ourselves.

It was great fun when the pigs were collected.

Fat Mr Grau came with a big trailer. Unfortunately it didn't fit into the garden.

Dad said, well then, we'll have to drive the pigs out on to the street and put them into the trailer there.

I thought it was a pretty stupid idea from the beginning, but nobody listens to children. Because, if a pig sees a trailer, it immediately thinks, now I'm off to the **butcher's**. And it won't be so stupid as to climb in there on its own!

Dad and Mr Grau did everything wrong from the beginning. Grown-ups are really stupid sometimes. Instead of taking the pigs out of the basement one by one, they brought them all out at once.

Dirk and I watched.

The pigs left the basement one behind the other. They were excited because they'd never been outside and they were probably afraid as well. In any case, before they were

---

butcher's – Schlachter

properly on the street, they had started grunting like crazy and running around in all directions.

One of them was even more stupid than Dad and Mr Grau, because it ran straight into the trailer. Two of the others ran back into the garden and I closed the garden gate behind them.

But the last two galloped down the street.

One of them was the pig whose snout Björn had stuck his finger into. We had **christened** him Didi Dada. The other one was called Gertrud because it was just as fat as Mum's sister.

Didi Dada and Gertrud were unbelievably fast because they obviously thought they were about to be made into sausage.

Dad chased Didi Dada and Mr Grau followed Gertrud, and Dirk and I followed Dad and Mr Grau.

Mr Grau was even fatter than Gertrud but much quicker. His face was bright red and he gasped for breath and looked like a **steamroller**. He finally **caught up with** fat Gertrud and jumped on her with a dive. There was a brief struggle and Mr Grau and Gertrud both did a lot of grunting and wrestling on the street.

Dirk and I cheered Gertrud on, but sadly Mr Grau was stronger. He dragged poor, defeated Gertrud over to the

---

to christen – taufen
steamroller – Dampfwalze
to catch up with someone – jemanden einholen

trailer and screamed at us both that we were **traitors** and bloody pig lovers.

In the meantime Didi Dada had turned off into the Rieders' house on the other side of the street. They had lots of flowerbeds instead of a fence and a chicken coop in the garden at the back.

Didi Dada trampled a rose bed, then whizzed over the lawn and under Mrs Rieder's washing line, which had white bed sheets hanging from it that reached all the way down to the ground. Didi Dada tried to rush through but her snout got caught in one of the sheets and tore it off the line. It wrapped itself around her and Dida Dada couldn't see anything any more and had to stay where she was. Her little curly tail peeked out from under the sheet.

Dad was creeping up to her just as Dirk and I came around the corner and he would have been able to grab her if Mrs Rieder hadn't suddenly come out of the house.

She screamed and wanted to know what was going on.

Didi Dada got a fright, shook her head and the sheet slipped off. Now her snout was peeking out and one ear and one eye, and with her cape she looked like Superman. She **spied** Mrs Rieder and Dad and Dirk and I and ran off again in the direction of the chicken coop. But she didn't brake in time and thundered through the thin **mesh fence**

---

traitor – Verräter
to spy – *hier*: erblicken
mesh fence – Maschendrahtzaun

right into the middle of the coop. And then she sat down and gave up.

The chickens went wild and flew around and squawked and a few of them fled through the hole in the fence. There were a lot of feathers flying around.

In her bedsheet Didi Dada looked like a little iceberg covered in penguin poo with snow falling on it. She grunted unhappily. Dad climbed into the coop and picked her up.

When he came back out, Mrs Rieder shouted at him that he should take her bed sheets off the dirty pig immediately. She demanded **compensation** for the rosebed and the chicken coop and the fact that the chickens wouldn't be able to lay any eggs for at least a week because of the shock.

Dad shouted back that Mrs Rieder could take her sheet and **stuff it**, and the chicken coop too, and lay the stupid eggs herself, and then we all went back home while Mrs Rieder tried to catch her stupid chickens.

Dirk and I were quite sad when Didi Dada and her friends were all in the trailer and Mr Grau drove off with them. But Mum said she was happy that the stupid creatures had finally disappeared. She was cross because the two pigs that had been in the garden had trampled her newly laid lawn.

---

compensation – Schadenersatz
stuff it – *hier*: es sich an den Hut stecken

The pigsty was **torn down**.

Now all we needed was a new floor in the basement and Dad had borrowed a cement mixer and Uncle Alfred for that. Uncle Alfred was great at making concrete, but he was pretty stupid at everything else. He had once said that guinea pigs were his favourite food and he could swallow Fran down just like that and since then I hadn't been able to stand him.

But Dirk and I were allowed to help him, which was great. Björn played in the sand with a spade and some **moulds**.

To mix concrete you need sand and cement and water. You throw seven shovelfuls of sand and four shovelfuls of cement into the mixer and you pour two buckets of water in too. You mustn't put in too much or too little, or it won't work. The machine mixes everything and wham, bam, the concrete is ready.

When the concrete was ready we put it into a **wheelbarrow**. Uncle Alfred pushed it into the basement, shook it out and spread it properly while Dirk and I loaded up the next lot. When the whole cellar was full of concrete, I went upstairs to find Dad.

He was wallpapering the living room with Granny.

Granny had been a big help in the last few weeks. She

---

to tear something down – etwas abreißen
mould – *hier*: Förmchen
wheelbarrow – Schubkarre

was really enjoying it and said it was like after the war when she'd helped to clear away the **rubble**. The rubble women had cleared away the rubbish for months after everything had been **destroyed** by the bombs.

Granny had said that our house looked the way it did after the war and because of that Dad was cross with her.

That's why he was pleased that Granny was so afraid of the ladder. She had to climb up there to hold on to the wallpaper while Dad glued it on to the wall with a brush. Granny couldn't get down the ladder by herself. Dad had to help her because she was so fat and thought that if she made one wrong move she'd fall over.

Dad wobbled the ladder **on purpose** and said she would definitely break through the floor, shoot into the bedroom on the ground floor and from there on into the basement and then the whole house would probably collapse on top of her.

Granny said before that she'd fall on top of Dad and that would shut his cheeky mouth forever.

Dad was really pleased that we had already finished mixing the concrete. He said now we could take a break and he and Granny would be finished soon too and if Granny didn't fall on top of him, then we could eat dinner soon. That was when we heard Mum screaming.

---

rubble – Schutt
to destroy – zerstören
on purpose – mit Absicht

While we had been mixing concrete outside and Dad and Granny had been arguing, Mum had been sorting through the attic. We had already carried up some of the boxes from the old house that needed storing. That had been difficult because there was only a **folding staircase** leading up. And the attic wasn't particularly high, you could easily bang your head if you weren't careful.

Mum had taken a lamp with her because the attic was quite dark with only a small **skylight**. And while she was clearing up she thought she might just peek out and see what she could see. So she had **squeezed** herself through the skylight and at first everything was fine. Mum could see Mr Grau's house and Mrs Rieder's chicken coop which had now been repaired. And she could see the other neighbours' houses and a bit of the woods and the town. And then she wanted to get down and she couldn't.

She was stuck in the skylight.

At first she had jiggled around a bit, but **it was no use**. That's why she had started to scream.

Dad and I rushed up the folding stairs at once. Uncle Alfred had heard Mum screaming from the basement and he bombed up the stairs with Dirk. Granny couldn't follow because she was standing on the ladder holding on to the wallpaper.

---

folding staircase – ausklappbare Treppe
skylight – Dachluke
to squeeze – quetschen
it was no use – es hatte keinen Sinn

We all squeezed into the attic. Dad pulled on Mum's legs which were peeking out of the skylight and he yelled at Uncle Alfred to join in.

But Uncle Alfred had banged his head and was cross and Mum shouted from outside that Dad shouldn't let Uncle Alfred near her legs and then he got even crosser and called, that's a nice thank you for mixing concrete!

Mum said he should shut his mouth because she had other problems, for example that her large bosom wouldn't fit through the skylight.

Uncle Alfred called back that he cared about her stupid bosom even less than her legs, he'd always known that Mum couldn't stand him. Dad asked if they could be a bit louder so that all the neighbours could hear and suddenly Mum fell down.

She landed right on top of Dad. Dad gasped for breath and coughed that Granny might just as well have fallen on top of him because she certainly couldn't be any heavier than Mum. And Mum got really angry and said she was **fed up** and her bosom hurt and she wanted to go home.

Then she looked at us all and asked where Björn was.

And then we all looked at each other and we ran back down the stairs and out into the garden and over to the pile of sand. That's where Uncle Alfred and Dirk had left Björn.

---

to be fed up – die Nase voll haben

But Björn wasn't there any more. There was only his little spade.

Mum started to cry and screamed at Uncle Alfred that he was an idiot and would have her missing son on his conscience and Uncle Alfred **lost it**. We all called Björn's name but there was no reply.

I thought about what I would have done if I'd been Björn and I looked in the basement. And there he was. He had crawled right through the concrete and made really deep impressions in it. Then he had sat in one corner and tried to make shapes with the stuff and that's where he'd been sitting for quite a long time. The concrete had gone all hard and Björn was **sealed in** by his bottom. But he was in a good mood and he was laughing and you could see his new milk teeth.

Dad wanted to fetch a **jackhammer** but Uncle Alfred said he shouldn't go over the top. The two of them fetched two ordinary hammers and began to chip away at the concrete.

Mum was still crying and said that Björn would definitely have a **bladder infection** from the cold concrete and he'd probably wet the bed for the rest of his life and it was all Uncle Alfred's fault.

---

to lose it – *umgangssprachlich*: ausrasten
to be sealed in – *hier*: einbetoniert sein
jackhammer – Presslufthammer
bladder infection – Blasenentzündung

They were able to free him quite quickly and Björn looked funny because there were lots of little grey pieces sticking to his bottom and his legs.

Mum said she wanted to go home immediately because Björn needed a hot bath.

It was dark already and we were all hungry. So we **traipsed** out of the basement, got into the car and drove home. We had already packed up so much stuff it looked as though we were moving right there and then. It was almost like being on a camping holiday. Mum gave Björn a bath and fed him and put him to bed and then she made hot soup.

And then she asked, where's Granny?

Dad went all pale.

We had left Granny standing on the ladder.

---

to traipse – latschen

The Rain in Spain

Ten weeks later, on a day with lovely weather, we moved house.

Dad had been **messing round** with the **plumbing** in the bathroom at the new house since early that morning because something wasn't working properly. Granny was there too, cleaning. Mum and Björn and Dirk and I were waiting for the moving van and the moving men at the old house.

They came driving down the road with their van. There was a tall **skinny** man and a small fat one next to him behind the steering wheel. The fat man's face was full of stubble and he was wearing a hat.

The two of them got out and the thin one shook Mum's hand and said, 'ello there, I'm Detlef and the man in the van is my pal Ernie. Now show us what you want **shifting**.

---

to mess around – herumwursteln
plumbing – *hier*: Rohrleitungen
skinny – mager
to shift – *hier*: schleppen

Detlef and Ernie fetched belts and blankets from the back of the van. Dirk and I watched them.

Ernie said to Dirk, 'ello little man, do you want to be a moving man when you grow up?

Dirk looked at Ernie and said, if that means I look and talk as strangely as you do, then probably not.

Mum said, Dirk! But Ernie and Detlef thought it was **hilarious** and got to work.

By lunchtime we were finished. Everything had been packed into the moving van and Ernie and Detlef got in and drove off. Mum locked the front door and I had a funny feeling in my stomach because I knew that we would never come back here again. Mum found it strange too and I think she even cried a little bit when we got into our car and drove after the moving van.

Dirk and I turned around and watched the house **dis-appear** behind the curve. I nearly cried too. Nobody said anything, even Björn was quiet in his baby seat. Only Toby squeaked and ran up and down in his cage, which was sitting on my lap.

When we arrived at the new house, Mrs Pankel came over to talk to Mum.

Mrs Pankel was a widow and lived right above us. She was as old as Granny, but a real **loony**. She spent the whole

---

hilarious – zum Totlachen
to disappear – verschwinden
a loony – ein Verrückter /eine Verrückte

day digging around in her flower and vegetable beds talking nonsense and singing strange songs, such as: *Black is the colour of my true love's hair.*

A proper loony.

Mrs Pankel was standing at the fence with a colourful cloth tied around her hair. She was wearing pink plastic gloves and green wellies. She was holding a small garden **hoe** in one hand.

She said to Mum that from her tomato plants she could see through the big window in our stairway and how nice it was with the new wallpaper. Could you get that wallpaper with a **vegetable pattern**, she asked, and would Mum like some tomatoes?

Granny always said that Mum was really good at dealing with people who were not quite right in the head because otherwise she wouldn't have married Dad. In any case, Mum said to Mrs Pankel that it was very kind of her to give us some tomatoes but we would eat them and not stick them on the wallpaper. And Mrs Pankel said, of course, of course, not until spring, then the tomatoes would stick to the wallpaper more easily.

A proper loony.

I went in to find Dad in the small bathroom and told him that the moving van had arrived.

---

hoe – Hacke
vegetable pattern – Gemüsemuster

Dad grumbled that he didn't have time but that Granny could help. He was lying on the floor half under the basin fiddling with a **pipe** that was sticking out of the wall using a small tool. Granny was standing there watching him with a cleaning cloth in one hand and a hammer in the other.

Dad looked really **irritated**. He had incredibly oily black hands and as he fiddled with the pipe using a large **pair of pliers**, he was swearing that it was a stupid rusty thing and one day the pipe would just burst.

Granny wiped the sink with the cloth and started to tell us how she had had to fetch water for cooking and washing with buckets from a well after the war, that was God's truth, it had been 200 metres away from the house and how everything was so easy these days with plumbing.

Dad grunted that Granny should hit the pliers with the hammer.

Granny hit him hard on the thumb with the hammer.

Dad screamed and banged his head on the sink.

He dropped the pliers and Granny said, in those days, after the war, it was difficult to get tools, you had to do everything with your bare hands, that was God's truth, and that Dad should be a bit more careful so that he didn't put a hole in the expensive new sink with his thick head.

---

pipe – Rohr
to be irritated – genervt sein
pair of pliers – Zange

Dad looked up at Granny from under the sink and said, if she didn't **vanish** from the bathroom immediately with her smelly cleaning cloth, he would give her a good slap over the head with it, that was God's truth.

Granny took a deep breath, dropped the hammer and marched out of the bathroom, insulted.

Good grief, Dad **whinged**, that woman will drive me crazy with her **natter**, and he wished he'd left Granny to starve last week on the ladder. Then he carried on screwing in the pipe.

Mum was holding Björn in the hallway, waiting for the two moving men so she could show them where to put the pieces of furniture. I followed Granny outside to help Dirk carry the smaller boxes.

Detlef and Ernie came towards us in the garden. They were carrying the living-room cupboard with the big top piece that you couldn't take off because it was glued on.

This'll be a problem, Ernie coughed, it's **a tad** too big.

Mrs Pankel was still standing by the fence watching Dirk carry boxes out of the van and put them down in a row on the pavement.

She called out to Granny that she had very nice, hard-working grandchildren and Granny said, yes, they got it

---

to vanish – verschwinden
to whinge – jammern
natter – Geschwätz
a tad – ein bisschen

from their mother. Because if we were like our shameless father, then we be stuck in a **young offenders' institution** and get into fights three times a day.

Then Granny climbed into the moving van and Mrs Pankel nodded and said, oh yes, the youth of today, and that she would go and pick some tomatoes for Mum now. She started singing, *To pull wild mountain thyme all around the blooming heather,* la la la. Dirk looked over at her crawling through her tomato bushes with her bottom sticking up in the air, la la la. He shook his head and rolled his eyes.

Dirk thinks tomatoes are just as disgusting as I do.

We followed Ernie and Detlef into the hallway with some boxes. The two of them were in the middle of carrying the cupboard up the stairs into the living room.

Ernie was already sweating and was saying to Detlef, oh crikey, if we could only take off the top bit, but it's stuck tight.

They heaved the cupboard up the first set of stairs until they reached the large window where there was a bend and the second set of stairs began. Then it got difficult, the stairs got narrower from that point on because the stairway was so narrow and the cupboard didn't really fit.

Mum had put Björn down in the hallway and he sat there with his rubber duck on the floor. She, Dirk and I put the boxes down and watched Detlef pulling at the cup-

---

young offenders' institution – Heim für schwer erziehbare Jugendliche

board from above and Ernie pushing it from below until they couldn't move any more.

Ernie's face was bright red from all the **effort**. He pushed his cap back, looked up at Detlef past the cupboard and said, **there's no point**, Detlef! I'll put **meself** in between the piece of furniture and the **banisters**, then you can push it to the side a bit, all right?

It was great the way Ernie sucked in his fat stomach and squeezed himself into a hole where only Björn could really have fit. I had to **giggle**. Dirk and Mum made funny faces too because Ernie's bottom spilled out of the banisters.

Ernie gave two short coughs, pushed the cupboard up a bit and then he said, that's it, what a mess, now I'm stuck here, I don't believe it!

Detlef said, I don't believe it either, how can a grown man be so stupid, I should leave yer where yer are, mate!

And then he started pushing the cupboard from above instead of pulling it.

Mum asked if the cupboard would slide down the stairs if Ernie managed to get his stomach out. Detlef said, lady, are you trying to tell an **experienced mover** how to do his job, or what?

---

effort – Anstrengung
there's no point – es hat keinen Zweck
meself – *umgangssprachlich für*: myself – mich
banister – Geländer
to giggle – kichern
experienced mover – erfahrener Möbelpacker

Then he called out, Ernie, **suck yer bloody stomach in a bit** and hold yer breath so I can push this down a bit more.

Ernie's face got even redder when he held his breath and so did Detlef's as he pushed and made strange noises. It was really exciting, that's why we didn't notice Granny until she was already standing in the hallway calling Mum's name in a really high-pitched voice.

We looked down at Granny and at first I thought she had pulled one of the moving boxes over her head. From above she looked like she had four corners. But it wasn't a box, it was our shoe cupboard which Granny had loaded on to her back.

She was bent right over in the middle of the hallway **screeching** that she had pulled her back and couldn't move. Björn was trying to pull himself up on her legs so that he could stand and Granny began to wobble and **wheezed** that she had a pain in her chest and that she was going to have a heart attack.

Mum screamed, for God's sake, Mum, don't drop that thing on Björn!

She was just about to run down the stairs when the banister behind Ernie suddenly cracked. Then it snapped and moved a little bit.

---

suck yer bloody stomach in a bit – *umgangssprachlich*: zieh deinen fetten Bauch ein bisschen ein
to screech – kreischen
to wheeze – keuchen

Ernie shrieked, dropped the cupboard and waved his arms around like crazy to keep his balance. Mum jumped forward and pushed Ernie's fat behind through the banisters on the staircase.

Detlef cried from above, Ernie, don't drop the thing, there'll be an accident!

But then it was too late.

The cupboard thundered down the stairs and crashed against the wall right under the window on the landing. The force of the collision was so great that the top bit broke off, shot through the window pane and sailed outside. There was **a clatter and a clang**, then a **muffled** crash and a scream.

The crash was made by the top part of the cupboard as it landed in Mrs Pankel's vegetable patch, and the scream came from Mrs Pankel who had been crawling around in between her tomato bushes.

Granny screamed from below that she was having her heart attack now and the shoe cupboard was starting to slide and Dad shouted out from the bathroom, what was going on out there again in this madhouse.

Detlef shouted back, come out, everybody's being squashed and that neighbour of yers, the crazy lady, she's got the piece of furniture **on 'er noggin**.

---

a clatter and a clang – ein Klirren und Scheppern
muffled – dumpf
on 'er noggin – *umgangssprachlich*: auf ihre Birne

Dirk and Mum and I pushed frantically against Ernie's bottom and Detlef tugged on his arms from above.

Down below Dad stormed out of the bathroom and arrived just in time to catch the stupid shoe cupboard before it fell on Björn.

Detlef had pulled Ernie completely on to the stairs and Mum was coughing, my God, Mrs Pankel, and everybody rushed down the stairs past Granny and into the garden.

Mrs Pankel was lying flat on her back with her green wellies in the air behind the fence. Right next to her the top part of the cupboard had embedded itself in the ground and everything was red.

For a moment I thought Mrs Pankel was dead and was lying in her own blood, but it was only the squashed tomatoes. And then I heard Mrs Pankel singing softly that the rain in Spain falls gently on the plain or something like that.

Ernie whispered, the shock has sent her mad, the old girl, Mrs Pankel must have thought a UFO was landing in her garden.

Detlef said, rubbish, she was **a few sandwiches short of a picnic** beforehand, the old girl, or did Ernie think he'd burst into song if aliens were landing in his garden?

Mum ran to the fence and called, Mrs Pankel, Mrs Pankel, and had something happened to her.

---

to be a few sandwiches short of a picnic – nicht alle Tassen im Schrank haben

Mrs Pankel stopped singing and sat up. Her headscarf had slipped over one eye and she looked like the captain of a pirate ship.

She smiled at Mum and asked how the tomatoes had tasted and when the children were coming home from the young offenders' institution. Then she jumped up and started hacking away at the top part of the cupboard with her hoe.

Dad said, she needs to go to a doctor, old Pankel, before she starts hacking away at her own head with the hoe, and anyway, Ernie and Detlef should pick up the top part of the cupboard before she turns it all into firewood.

The two of them climbed over the fence and stomped through the squashed tomatoes. Right, lady, Ernie said to Mrs Pankel, let's put down the hoe, shall we, so that we can take this thing out of your **veggies**, eh?

Mrs Pankel looked at Detlef, put her hoe to one side and said, ah, what a charming young man and could she invite him over for tea.

Dad looked at Mum and whispered, if he hadn't already known old Pankel was crazy, he'd think the top of the cupboard had done it.

Dirk said, that's mean of everybody to say that Mrs Pankel isn't quite right in the head. She's a lovely old granny and Mum called, oh bloody hell, we've forgotten Granny again!

---

veggies – *umgangssprachlich für*: Gemüse

She ran into the house and Dad, Dirk and I ran after her.

Granny was still standing bent over in the corridor because of her pulled back and was grumbling that nobody could care less if she died of a heart attack or not. Mum should call a doctor immediately and take Björn away because he was tickling her **calves**.

Dad picked up Björn and thought it might be better if Ernie and Detlef carried Granny outside into the moving van and took her to hospital and took Mrs Pankel with them too to be on the safe side.

Granny got cross and said, if Dad shut her in the van with that loony woman, she would **disinherit** the whole family and make sure we would all have to **live off benefits**.

Dad said, right then, let's fetch the doctor. But Granny would have to move out of the hallway because she was in the way.

Dirk said, we could make Granny wear a red woolly hat and put her in the flowerbed like a garden gnome until the doctor comes and I started to laugh.

Granny was just about to start grumbling again when a strange noise came from the bathroom. Dad passed Björn to me, ran into the bathroom and shot out again immediately.

---

calves – Waden
to disinherit someone – jemanden enterben
to live off benefits – von Sozialhilfe leben

The pipe's about to blow, he shouted. He had to go straight to the basement to turn off the water at the mains.

And he would have been able to if Ernie and Detlef hadn't staggered into the entrance to the hallway carrying the top part of the cupboard and blocked his way.

Dad screamed, make way, and took a huge **leap** over the cupboard.

What on earth was that, Ernie asked looking at him, Superman or what?

Granny said that was her idiotic **son-in-law** and if there was any justice in heaven, he'd fall down the stairs to the basement and land on his **cheeky gob**.

Mum said, Mum, not in front of the children!

Lady, don't be so horrible, Ernie said, why don't you just move out the way.

She would like to, said Granny, but she couldn't move, and nobody in this house could care less and that's why she couldn't care less about the stupid cupboard or about anything else, apart from the pipe because the water might ruin her **perm**.

Good grief, Mum said, I'll call the doctor and then she murmured that this was another one of those days when she felt very old.

---

the pipe's about to blow – das Rohr bricht gleich
leap – Sprung
son-in-law – Schwiegersohn
cheeky gob – freches Maul
perm – Dauerwelle

At that moment Dad came up from the basement. He wiped the sweat from his brow and said, everything's OK, but if anything else happened that didn't usually happen to normal people, he'd start screaming and never stop again.

And then we heard a voice from outside singing *Cape Cod girls ain't got no combs*, and Mrs Pankel appeared in the doorway behind Dad. She was wearing a straw hat with plastic cherries on it and she was carrying a tray with a steaming pot of tea and teacups and biscuits on it. She smiled at Dad and said, right my dears, the tea's ready, now let's make ourselves cosy before we all have to go back to the young offenders' institution!

The Mudwrestlers

When we had finally moved into the new house, Dad said, right, the children are still on summer holidays and I'm off too, so let's all have a week's holiday at the Edersee.

We had a **caravan** with a tent attached parked on a campsite at the Edersee. In summer we usually drove out there every weekend. But because of the renovations and the move we hadn't managed to go yet this year even though it was only an hour away in the car.

Dirk and I were really looking forward to it, but Mum started to grumble.

She said, what a great idea! It made no difference whether she cleaned up our dirty washing and everything else at home or in a small caravan while Dad clowned around singing with his fishing pals by the campfire. And how nice it would be because Uncle Alfred would be there with Erika too, so Uncle Alfred could try and **grope** Mum for a whole week with his fat sausage fingers.

---

caravan – Wohnwagen
to grope – begrapschen

Uncle Alfred and Aunt Erika had a caravan at the campsite too, really close to us, and they were there every weekend.

At first I thought Mum was serious but then she laughed and said, all right boys, we can go on Friday.

But in fact we started on Thursday, because we needed to put up the **tent extension** and do all kinds of other things and Dad wanted everything to be done by Friday when his fishing friends arrived at the Edersee for the weekend.

There was a lot to pack and we had to go shopping too. Mum **muttered** to herself while she was pushing the shopping trolley through the supermarket and while we were packing the car she was still grumbling. She said, it was typical Dad rushing from one move to the next and he did it all on purpose so that she would get as many wrinkles and grey hairs as possible in the shortest period of time so that no other man would ever look at her, apart from Uncle Alfred of course, the old groper.

When we left, late in the afternoon, the car looked as though we were emigrating to America rather than just going to the Edersee for a week. Everything was **crammed full of stuff**, the **roof rack** and the **boot** and wherever there was space. There was even a lot of stuff on the back

---

tent extension – Vorzelt
to mutter – murren
to be crammed full of stuff – mit Zeug vollgestopft sein
roof rack – Dachgepäckträger
boot – *hier*: Kofferraum

seat where Dirk and I were sitting with Fran on our lap and Björn in his baby seat. It was a real squeeze. We were already uncomfortable after fifteen minutes in the car.

I thought, this is how a sardine in a **tin** must feel, squashed like this, only it's dead of course and so it can't complain any more.

I said that to Dirk and he thought about it, about him and dead sardines and then he said, a little bit of him was also squashed and dead because I'd been sitting on his left hand since we left.

It was a stupid drive. When we set off the sun was still shining, but after a while there were clouds everywhere and it looked as thought it was going to rain. We were bored.

Then Björn filled his nappy and it stank of carrots and I was really happy when we arrived at the campsite.

By then the sky had gone grey and dark and the first raindrops were splashing down on to the car.

Dad parked on the narrow path right in front of our caravan so that we didn't have too far to walk with all our stuff. He was in a really good mood and called out, everybody on board and let's get down to work.

Mum said maybe it wasn't such a good idea to put up the tent extension just yet in case the rain got heavier.

But Dad said, typical woman, letting herself be **put off by** a few drops of rain! Of course we would put the tent up

---

tin – Büchse

to be put off by something – *hier*: sich durch etwas abhalten lassen now, Madam could sit herself down in the caravan with her youngest son and wait for better weather.

Mum said, Madam would remain seated in the car because the caravan needed airing and so did their youngest son and whether Sir would be so friendly as to dig the nappies out of the boot.

Dad, Dirk and I got out and went to the boot. First of all we took out the big **canvas** and the poles for the tent. I carried them over to the caravan with Dad. We threw everything on to the wooden floor where the tent stands when it's finished.

Dirk rummaged around for the nappy bag and when he'd found it and given it to Mum, he followed us.

Putting up an extension tent isn't easy because you have to attach one side of it to the caravan. You have to fasten the tent poles firmly to the caravan and to the wooden floor so that the tent doesn't fall over. First the poles have to be attached to one another to make a frame, but Dad had done it lots of times already so it didn't take long. By the time Mum had changed Björn's nappy, nearly the entire frame was up, but we hadn't fastened it to the caravan yet.

Now it was really windy and the rain was getting heavier.

Mum got out of the car and ran over to us. She said, fabulous, there's bound to be a **thunderstorm**.

---

canvas – Zeltplane
thunderstorm – Gewitter

Dad said, rubbish, if there was going to be a storm then he'd be the first to know because the scar from his stomach operation would start **itching.**

Dirk asked, what kind of operation, and Dad answered, the one from his **stomach ulcer.**

Dirk asked him, what's a stomach ulcer, and just then there was a flash of lightning and a few seconds later the thunder started.

Mum called, see, there's the storm. There was another flash of lightning and she asked Dad if his scar had started to itch yet.

Dad said, no, it hadn't, but it would soon because his scar was also **sensitive to** annoying women.

Dirk tugged at Dad's shirt sleeve and wanted to know what a stomach ulcer was when the next lot of thunder came and Dad suddenly shouted that a stomach ulcer is something you get when you **get wound up** about certain women who always think they're right and about children who ask stupid questions and it was a miracle that he had put up with this family for so long without having had to have a heart operation as well!

Then he put the last tent pole in place and said, chop chop, we've got to throw the canvas over the frame and fasten it before we can fasten the poles to the ground.

---

to itch – jucken
stomach ulcer – Magengeschwür
to be sensitive to something – auf etwas empfindlich reagieren
to get wound up about something – sich über etwas aufregen

The wind got stronger and stronger. There was thunder and lightning and the rain poured down on us and we were all soaking wet.

Mum looked up and said that the heavens had really opened and that it would be better to stop, and she wouldn't be surprised if the wind picked up too.

Dad looked at Mum and shouted that he wouldn't be surprised if she **drove him mad** with her stupid comments. She should join in and help instead of pretending that she was the **weather fairy**.

So Mum joined in.

She and Dad unrolled the canvas quickly and threw it over the poles and Dad said to Mum, you see, Madam, that's how's quick it can be if you do it properly and the storm could come whenever it liked.

Mum wiped the wet hair out her face and then she looked at Dad and said, then maybe it would be better to put the canvas on the right way round before the storm arrived.

And she was right, the canvas was the wrong way round, with the inside on the outside.

I didn't think it mattered all that much because with all the rain it was better than nothing but Dad jumped around like **Rumpelstiltskin** and tried to take the canvas off the

---

to drive someone mad – jemanden wahnsinnig machen
weather fairy – Wetterfee
Rumpelstiltskin – Rumpelstilzchen

poles and he shouted at Dirk and I not to stand around doing nothing but **to give him a hand.**

The wind was really strong now. The canvas blew up at the sides and fluttered like mad, and Dirk and I jumped through the mud and tried to catch the ends. Everything started to wobble because the poles weren't fastened to the ground and even a blind man could see that it wasn't going to end well.

Mum cried out, good grief, Peter, leave the canvas where it is and get back into the car with the children!

But Dad kept on pulling at the tent and shouted at the canvas that it was a stupid piece of material, he wouldn't let himself be **brought to his knees** by a piece of plastic and that he would soon show it who was boss.

Mum had to hold on to a few poles because they were moving to the side. Dirk and I held on to something too, but I can't remember what because everything was so chaotic.

And suddenly somebody **honked a car horn**.

At first I thought that Björn had got bored and started playing in the car and had managed to reach the horn.

But it wasn't Björn. It was old Johann with Elfriede and their dachshund Sissi. They were standing behind our car in their rusty old banger and couldn't get past.

---

pole – Stange
to give someone a hand – jemandem helfen
to be brought to one's knees by something – sich von etwas fertigmachen lassen
to honk a car horn – hupen

Mum said, that too, that was all that had been missing, and Johann probably wanted to get to his caravan. It was the one right next to ours and Johann and Elfriede were our **enemies**. They couldn't stand us and they were always **complaining** about something because Dirk and I had once put a pair of my underpants on Sissi and tied a ribbon around her tail and put a hat on her because we wanted to play mums and dads.

In any case, now they were standing there in the storm and Johann wouldn't stop honking his horn.

Dad shouted that the old man wasn't quite right in the head, he could see that we couldn't move our car at the moment because otherwise the tent would fly off!

I looked at our car and I could see Björn standing on the back seat banging his little hands on the window crying because he was afraid of the storm and Johann's honking.

Mum had seen him too and shouted at Dad, that's really enough, she was going to get Björn and she couldn't care less whether the tent collapsed or not.

She let go of the poles and ran through the rain to the car. The tent began to wobble straight away.

Dad screamed after Mum that she should at least move the car so that that idiot Johann would finally stop his **racket**.

---

enemy – Feind
to complain – sich beschweren
racket – *hier*: Lärm

Mum would have done that but she couldn't because Björn had pressed down all the buttons on the doors and the key was still in the **ignition**. Mum made signals with her arms in front of the windscreen to show Björn how to open a door, but Björn was busy crying and when he cried he didn't care about anything else.

Mum screamed, bloody hell and Dad should come to the car right away because his youngest son was in difficulty.

But Dad was in difficulty himself because the poles that Mum had been holding suddenly **upended** and now there was nothing to be done and the whole tent collapsed. The only pole that was still standing was the one that Dirk and I were holding.

Dirk splashed around in a puddle and sang *Raindrops keep falling on my head* and I think Dad would have clocked him if he hadn't been busy fighting with the canvas. It looked like a giant flying carpet flying up and down on all sides.

Mum screamed that she didn't believe it and then Johann honked his horn again.

If Johann had known Mum, then he would have known that it was better not to wind her up if she was worried about Björn. As quick as a flash she was standing next to his car door and had torn it open and right away the storm pushed rain into Johann's face. Elfriede's eyes were as large as saucers.

---

ignition – Zündschloss
to upend – umkippen

Mum screamed at them right away, before the two of them could even say anything, that she would destroy their set of wheels and turn their stupid little dog into fish food if Johann didn't stop honking his horn immediately.

And so that he saw she meant it seriously, she put a big **dent** in the car door with her left foot.

I thought, now Johann will have a heart attack. Not because of the dent, but because Sissi had jumped over his lap and out of the car.

Elfriede screamed, my Sissi-poo, and she tore open her door and jumped out of the car.

Sissi ran under our caravan, Elfriede threw herself into the mud and crept after her and her legs stuck out and you could see her underskirt.

Johann roared at Mum, I'll report you to the police for that dent and then you and your **cheeky brood** will land **behind bars** where you belong!

Mum laughed and shouted, ha, I'll give you bars, and she grabbed one of the windscreen wipers and bent it in half.

Johann leapt out of the car.

Mum said, make one false move and I'll hit you over the head, you mean old man, and that was exactly the moment when Dad fell over Elfriede's leg.

---

dent – Beule
cheeky brood – freche Brut
behind bars – hinter Gittern

He hadn't seen her because he'd been wrapped up in the tent canvas and he looked like an Egyptian mummy. The only things that weren't in the canvas were his hands and with those he groped at Elfriede's bottom and **tugged** at her underskirt.

Johann roared at Dad that he should take his fingers off his wife and he ran past Mum and threw himself at Dad and Mum threw herself at Johann and hit him a few times.

I would have liked to have joined in but there was already such chaos in the mud that you couldn't really see who was who and that's why I just watched and cheered on Mum and Dad. Dirk stood next to me. He was still holding the tent pole tightly and this time he sang *Way-ay blow the man down* and it was fantastic.

Sissi had come out of the other side of the caravan and sat down next to Dirk and I. The rain was pouring down on us and mud **splattered** everywhere from the fighting. There was thunder and lightning. Now and again there was a rattling when Elfriede or Dad banged their head under the caravan or when Mum gave Johann a whack.

I think that Sissi was thinking the same as me, which was that grown-ups are sometimes worse than little children, especially when they fight.

Later we all sat in Johann's caravan and Dad and Johann got drunk on grog.

---

to tug – ziehen
to splatter – spritzen

I don't understand it. Grown-ups are strange. A minute ago they had been rolling around in the dirt like pigs, hitting each other and then suddenly they had stopped and everybody looked at each other and started to laugh.

Mum had gone to the car and she looked great. She was brown all over with mud which the rain was slowly washing off. **At some point** Björn had stopped crying and finally opened one of the car doors and Mum took him out and held him. Fran had missed everything, he was lying in his cage **snoozing.**

Björn had **snot** sticking to his face and Elfriede said, isn't that cute, the dirty little monkey! She herself looked as though she'd won the first prize in a competition for the best mudwrestler at the Edersee.

Dad and Johann were still laughing and clapping themselves on the back and the mud sprayed everywhere and Dad didn't stop laughing even when he noticed that he had left the keys to our caravan at home.

Right then, said Johann, we should all go over to their caravan. And that's where we were, in Johann and Elfriede's large caravan, wet and filthy.

Elfriede had made hot chocolate. That's for the little ones because they're so sweet, she said, and she and Mum drank tea and Dad and Johann drank grog.

---

at some point – irgendwann
to snooze – schlummern
snot – Rotz

Dirk had to sing *Way-ay blow the man down* again and everybody sang along, and Mum put one of Björn's nappies and his summer cap on Sissi and hung Björn's **dummy** around her and we sat there together for a long time, singing sea shanties and **having a really good laugh.**

---

dummy – *hier*: Schnuller
to have a really good laugh – einen Riesenspaß haben

Agathe's Big Journey

The sun beat down from the sky. It was really hot and it was really busy on the **platform**.

Kids were running around excitedly and Mum stood with the other mums and cried because she had to say goodbye, as though she wouldn't see me again for years. A few of the other mums cried too. Only the dads didn't **dare**.

But the school trip was only for a week.

I was standing next to my large bag full of clothes, carrying my small green rucksack. I was really cross because I wasn't allowed to take any Coke with me, only yukky tea with no sugar. And on top of everything the tea was in a small plastic bottle with a picture of **Little Red Riding Hood** on it.

That's for babies, Dirk said, and grinned.

I didn't say anything. He was just cross because he wasn't going on a school trip.

---

platform – Bahnsteig
to dare – sich trauen
Little Red Riding Hood – Rotkäppchen

We were going to spend a week with Miss Weide and Mr Holm, the sports teacher, in Ulm.

Ulm is a city somewhere left and at the bottom on the map. There's a church there called the Ulm Minster, and there are mountains all around called the Swabian Alps and we were going to climb both of them. And there would also be *Spätzle* and *Maultaschen*, the first one was a kind of noodle and the second one was a regional speciality, Miss Weide had said. Probably what we would get when we had finished all the stupid climbing.

Minsters and silly mountains and *Spätzle* and *Maultaschen*!

I thought the whole idea was stupid. You could go climbing near where we lived, on the Schlossberg. We had our own church too and there was always enough to eat. If we had to go on a school trip, then we could at least have gone to Africa or the North Sea, I thought. Susanne had **suggested** that we go to Disneyland in America and visit Mickey Mouse, but that was too expensive for Miss Weide.

There was nothing to be done, we had to go to Ulm.

Miss Weide had stood in the classroom and said, in Ulm, around Ulm and around about Ulm, we were sure to have a lot of fun, ha ha, and she had fiddled with her necklace the way she always did. Then she had said, dear Mr Holm is coming along too.

---

to suggest – vorschlagen

Behruz and Uli **groaned** out loud.

They liked the idea of *Maultaschen* and the *Spätzle*-things of course. But Mr Holm only had sports on the brain, he would certainly want to go climbing all the time. In the break Behruz said, we'll spend all day going up and down mountains, up and down, and in the end he would **faint** and miss all the *Maultaschen*.

Uli stood next to Behruz and nodded. Since the two of them had jumped into the rescue net together last year they had been the best of friends.

In any case, now we were standing around on the platform waiting for the train and I was carrying the stupid bottle with the red cap with tea but no sugar.

You're the only one here with such a stupid bottle, Dirk said loudly. Everybody could hear him and everybody looked at me.

It was really embarrassing.

But then the train came. Miss Weide ran to and fro like an idiot so that nobody would be forgotten, and she pulled at her necklace and Mr Holm grinned at all the mums with his white sports teacher teeth.

Mum held me tight and was still crying. She said I should take care of myself and not to do anything stupid.

That's what almost all the mums and dads were saying to their children and I thought, we should be saying that to

---

to groan – stöhnen
to faint – in Ohnmacht fallen

our parents instead. Because if you don't keep an eye on them, they only **get up to mischief** and we're the ones left to clean up the mess cos in the end they get divorced like Christiane's parents.

Christiane's mum had brought her to the station by herself.

Dad gave me a kiss on the cheek and said, listen to your mum and don't get into any trouble, young man!

It's boring with no trouble, Dirk said.

But I barely heard that because I was already halfway on to the train. I really wanted to sit in the same **compartment** as Richard and Behruz and Uli and Susanne and Christiane.

There was an awful lot of pushing and shoving in the carriage and Miss Weide's voice called out from somewhere, children, make some space!

Uli squeezed his way down the narrow **aisle** from the back. He looked as though he'd put weight on because his stomach was bigger than usual. Behruz squeezed his way after him, swearing in Persian. Richard and I came from the other side, and Susanne and Christiane were already standing in front of an empty compartment that they were keeping free for us.

We threw all our bags and rucksacks inside and then we stood by the window and waved at our parents while the

---

to get up to mischief – Unsinn machen
compartment – Abteil
aisle – Gang

conductor blew the whistle and the train slowly pulled away.

Dirk shouted, have a good trip, have a good trip and then the train drove around a bend and we couldn't see anybody any more.

It was great in our compartment. We stashed our stuff in the **luggage nets** and then we pulled the seats out so that we had one big lounge area with lots of space. Susanne had brought lots of Mickey Mouse comics with her which she shared out among us and we unpacked our food and drinks and settled in.

Behruz drank my watery tea and gave each of us a really tasty meatball.

Susanne asked what the tasty things were.

Behruz said, it's a dewjay kebab.

Richard almost spat out his dewjay thingummy for laughing and called, what's that?

Dewjay kebab, Behruz said.

Great, said Uli, who had stuffed so much of the dewy stuff into his mouth that it almost fell out again when he started talking. And what's it made from?

Little chickens, Behruz said.

Christiane screamed and threw her dewjay away. It landed in the luggage net above her.

What do you mean, said Susanne, we're eating sweet little chickens?

---

luggage nets – Gepäcknetze

Behruz said they weren't sweet because before they went in the oven they were put in a spicy sauce and we shouldn't **make such a big deal out of it** because after all we did eat grown-up chickens.

That's right, I said, and their eggs too.

Christiane wanted to say something, but **she happened to glance** at Uli's stomach and started screaming again. If she had still had a dewjay, she would definitely have thrown the other one into the luggage net too.

Uli's stomach was moving. Something was crawling around under his T-shirt.

At that moment the compartment door opened and Miss Weide looked in. Well, children, she said, are you all getting along?

Uli quickly put his hands over his stomach.

We're just eating Persian noodle kebabs, said Richard and **beamed at** Miss Weide as though he was Mr Holm with his pearly white teeth.

Behruz and I beamed too.

Miss Weide tugged at her necklace and said, right, yes, and that she only wanted to tell us that we would arrive in three hours and until then we should behave ourselves and keep our hands off the **emergency brakes**, ha ha, tug tug.

Susanne said, OK, and stared at Uli's stomach.

---

to make a big deal out of something – ein Drama aus etwas machen
she happened to glance – sie blickte zufällig
to beam at someone – jemanden anstrahlen
emergency brake – Notbremse

Miss Weide closed the compartment door again.

For five seconds it was really quiet. Then we all started shouting and wanted to know what Uli had hidden under his T-shirt.

This, said Uli and pulled up his shirt, is Agathe!

A **tortoise** was sitting on Uli's wobbly belly moving its funny little legs around. It was quite small, about fifteen centimetres long, and it looked great with its shiny shell and its stubby nose and little tail peeking out from underneath it.

We were **flabbergasted**.

A proper tortoise, Christiane whispered.

There'll be trouble, Behruz said, if Holm or Weide see it. It'll end up in a soup.

Richard asked why Uli had brought the tortoise along and Susanne asked, yes, why would you do a thing like that?

Stupid question, said Uli. A really stupid question. She wants to see the Ulm Minster of course.

The youth hostel where we were staying was great.

On the first day we had *Maultaschen* for lunch. *Maultaschen* means snoutpockets in German. I didn't know why they were called that because they didn't have a snout and they didn't look like pockets either, at least not properly. They were actually like giant ravioli, only not as **tasty**.

---

tortoise – Schildkröte
flabbergasted – entgeistert
tasty – lecker

But Behruz thought they were great and he stuck some of them in his trouser pockets, for later, he said.

When he tried to fish them out again that afternoon, they were completely squashed. Not even Agathe wanted to eat them mashed up. But she didn't go hungry because we'd arranged that we would steal something for her at every meal in the youth hostel. Tomatoes and lettuce and fruit.

Agathe was actually quite boring. She spent most of the time under Uli's **jumper**. I felt a bit sorry for her because she couldn't crawl around outside in the grass like she did at home. At night Uli put her in his bag to sleep.

Richard and Behruz and Uli and I had a room together on the second floor. The girls were in a separate room which I thought was stupid because it would have been great if Susanne and Christiane had slept in the same room as us.

But it was fun that way too.

On the second evening when we were supposed to be asleep, we had a **weeing competition** out of the window. We stood in pairs next to each other on the window ledge and the other two left over were the judges and had to say who had weed furthest and the most.

Behruz didn't want to join in at first because he was afraid of falling out of the window while he was weeing

---

jumper – *hier*: Pullover
weeing competition – Wettpinkeln

and then he would lie dead on the lawn with his trousers down.

But then he joined in after all and he even won, the idiot. He weed almost twice as far as Uli and for much longer than anybody else.

I promised myself that I would drink lots of tea tomorrow at dinner.

On the third day of our school trip we went to visit the Minster.

I thought it was great because the walls were really high and there were such beautiful things everywhere: giant colourful windows, statues made out of stone and even men made out of wood sitting on benches as though they were praying. They looked just as holy as the penguins did at home.

Miss Weide and Mr Holm walked around the church together and paid almost no attention to us.

After the visit we climbed one of the church towers, which had at least three million steps. Susanne felt sick when we reached the top and looked down. It was really windy and so high that when you spat down you couldn't see when your spit landed at the bottom. The houses and the cars and the people looked really tiny, like **ants**.

I promised myself – *hier*: ich nahm mir vor
to pray – beten
ants – Ameisen

Uli had brought Agathe along of course. He had hidden her under his jumper again and as we were standing on the tower, he brought her out and held her up in the air so that she could see everything. It was supposed to be her great moment, but I don't think Agathe thought it was all that great. She waved her legs around and pulled her head into her shell. She was probably afraid of falling.

Richard looked down at the city and said it would be much better to have a weeing competition from up here on the church tower instead of out of the window in the youth hostel.

Behruz thought it was a great idea. He had just undone his **flies** when Miss Weide came around the corner and stood next to us.

Isn't it lovely, children, she said, such a beautiful view, but Behruz should put away his willy wonka because we had to go back to the hostel. Then she looked up at the blue sky and seemed to be in a really good mood.

Behruz was so embarrassed that he looked as though he would prefer to jump off the church tower with his willy wonka. He fastened his flies with a bright red face and tried to whistle **nonchalantly**. Uli had stuffed Agathe back under his jumper really quickly.

Then we followed Miss Weide, who was humming a song, back down the hundreds of stairs.

---

flies – Hosenschlitz, Hosenstall
nonchalantly – unauffällig

On the fourth day, **things got sticky**. Miss Weide came into the dining room with Mr Holm at breakfast. She had bright red cheeks and was still in a good mood and didn't tug at her necklace once.

Dear children, she said, today we are finally going walking, to the Blue Pot.

And she explained that the Blue Pot was like a little lake with fantastically blue water somewhere far away from the youth hostel.

Christiane asked how far away the Blue Pot was and Mr Holm said, well, we do have to walk for a little bit. About fifteen kilometres. That's why we had all brought along our **walking gear** and we'd be setting off in half an hour.

Miss Weide smiled at Mr Holm and Mr Holm gave his sports teacher grin.

Susanne gasped for breath. If she hadn't taken out her braces before eating, it would definitely have fallen out of her mouth.

Fifteen kilometres, she gasped.

Thirty, there and back, said Christiane.

They're crazy, Holm and Weide, Richard whispered.

They're not crazy, said Susanne, they're in love and we're lucky they're not making us walk a hundred kilometres because lovers don't care.

---

things got sticky – *hier*: es wurde stressig
walking gear – Wanderkleidung

Behruz asked Susanne how she knew that they were in love.

Susanne looked at him as though he was one of the most stupid people in the world. Women can feel these things, she whispered. When two people were in love, there were **vibrations** in the air.

Behruz looked over at Miss Weide who was sitting next to Mr Holm and then he looked at Mr Holm and then at the air over the two of them.

There aren't any vibrations, he said to Susanne.

Wait for it, said Susanne, and stuck her braces back into her mouth.

Five hours later Uli was sitting on a **tree trunk** on the edge of the stupid pot that wasn't one bit blue complaining that he had **blisters** on his feet. He had put his rucksack with Agathe in it down on the ground next to him. His face was as red as a tomato from all the effort and he was sweating like crazy.

I thought the walk had been OK and so did Richard and Christiane. The sun was shining but there was a lot of wind and it wasn't too hot and insects were buzzing around. We had told each other jokes and sung songs with the other children from our class. And now and then we had watched Miss Weide and Mr Holm so as not to miss any vibrations.

---

vibrations – Schwingungen
tree trunk – Baumstumpf
blisters – Blasen

Mr Holm looked really **handsome** with his **knickerbocker walking shorts** and walking boots, and Miss Weide was wearing a funny little hat.

Behruz had been as grumpy on the way as Uli was now and an hour before we had arrived, Susanne had started to swear as well.

It was **torture**, this walking, she had snorted, and we could have been having a lovely time in Disneyland now, with Mickey Mouse and Baloo from the Jungle Book and all the rest of it! And that she would hit the next person who sang *I love to go a-wandering* on the nose.

Well, then we finally arrived at the Blue Pot and it was even more boring than Agathe. Just a big pool with a heap of water in it and a few empty Coke cans floating on top and woods all around.

Miss Weide thought it was great of course and Susanne said that Miss Weide was so in love that she would think a stinky **cesspit** was wonderful.

And then, just as Mr Holm had stepped away into the woods, it happened.

Uli got up from his tree trunk and hopped from one blistered foot to another and collided with his rucksack. There was a splash and the rucksack with Agathe inside was in the Blue Pot!

---

handsome – gutaussehend, stattlich
knickerbocker walking shorts – Kniebundhose
torture – Folter
cesspit – Klärgrube

Christiane screamed.

Uli screeched that Agathe would drown and that he couldn't swim and neither could Agathe because she was a land tortoise.

Miss Weide asked, what tortoise?

But then there was another splash and it was Behruz who had jumped in after the rucksack. The next splash came from Susanne who jumped in after Behruz and the next from Miss Weide who threw herself into the water after Susanne.

We all screamed like mad and ran around the Blue Pot and it looked really cool the way everybody was paddling through the pond.

Behruz had grabbed the rucksack and was holding it high above his head and Susanne had grabbed Behruz with a proper lifesaving grip and was pulling him to the bank. Richard helped the two of them climb out of the water.

Miss Weide could stand in the water because it only reached up as far as her chest and her pearl necklace floated around her neck. I had always **suspected** they weren't real pearls but that they were made out of wood or plastic instead. Miss Weide's small walking hat was floating on the water a few feet behind her.

When everybody was back on dry land and had shaken out their hair and Susanne had dried off her glasses with a

---

to suspect – vermuten, argwöhnen

tissue from Christiane, Mr Holm finally came running out of the woods.

Miss Weide threw herself into his arms, just like in a romantic film and drops of water sprayed in all directions. And then Mr Holm gave her a real kiss, **several** of them in fact, right on the mouth, and he said, Johanna, my darling, my love!

Uli fetched Agathe, who had got only a little wet, out of the rucksack. He held her right up in front of his face and said, Agathe, my darling, and gave her a kiss on the shell.

Everybody laughed themselves silly and then Mr Holm said, well, after this wet adventure we can't possibly walk back to the youth hostel and that he would walk to the next village and phone for a bus to come and pick us up.

That was a great idea!

When we had all climbed on the bus an hour later and were driving off, I looked over at the Blue Pot again where Miss Weide's little hat was still swimming around.

Thank God Miss Weide and Mr Holm weren't cross with Uli because of Agathe. She was even allowed to crawl around on the table at dinner and the cook from the hostel made her a special dinner of green lettuce.

After dinner we had an hour's free time before we had to go to bed. Richard and Uli and Christiane wanted to

---

tissue – *hier*: Taschentuch
several – einige

play table tennis so I took Agathe to our room to put her in her bag for the night.

I stroked her thick tortoise shell and she moved her little horned feet around. Dirk would have thought Agathe was great, I knew that. He liked all the same things I did. That's why he was the best brother in the world.

With Agathe in my arms I went over to the weeing competition window and looked out.

On the grass at the back of the hostel I could see Behruz sitting next to Susanne. They were holding hands and when Susanne gave Behruz a kiss on the **cheek**, I knew why she had jumped after him into the Blue Pot.

The air was full of vibrations …

---

cheek – Wange